The Definitive Biography of P.D.Q. Bach

(1807-1742)?

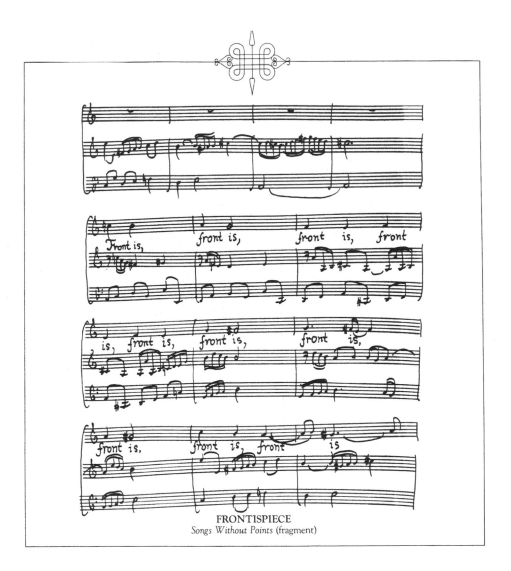

FRONTISPIECE
Songs Without Points (fragment)

Professor Peter Schickele

The Definitive Biography of P.D.Q. Bach

(1807-1742)?

Random House / New York

All rights reserved under International and Pan-American Copyright Conventions.
Published in the United States by Random House, Inc., New York,
and simultaneously in Canada by Random House
of Canada Limited, Toronto.

Library of Congress Cataloging in Publication Data

Schickele, Peter.
The definitive biography of P. D. Q. Bach.

1. Music—Anecdotes, facetiae, satire, etc.
2. Biography—Anecdotes, facetiae, satire, etc.
I. Title.
ML65.S34   813'.5'4   75-31682
ISBN 0-394-73409-2 (pbk)
ISBN 0-394-46536-9

Manufactured in the United States of America

Designed by Carole Lowenstein
BVG 01

Dedication

WOLFGANG AMADEUS MOZART
(1756-1791)

Why not?—What?—Why not?—Why should I not send it?—Why
should I not dispatch it?—Why not?—Strange! I don't know why I
shouldn't—Well, then—you will do me this favor.—Why
not?—Why should you not do it?—Why not?—Strange! I shall do
the same for you, when you want me to. Why not? Why should I
not do it for you? Strange! Why not?—I can't think why not?

—Letter to his cousin Maria

SPIKE JONES
(1911-1965)

Turn the page, ya fathead!

—*Glowworm*

Preface

"Why?" That is the question most often asked, by musicians and laypersons alike, after the concerts of P. D. Q. Bach's music presented by the author across the width and breadth of the North American continent. In the sixteen years that have elapsed since he began regularly performing the works of this musical missing link, the author estimates that that question, "WHY?" has been asked more than two thousand times in his presence; the number of times it has been asked behind his back, were it ascertainable, would surely boggle the mind, and a boggled mind is of no use to anyone. For that reason alone it would seem that providing some answers to this extraordinarily persistent question—probably the third most often-asked question in the Western hemisphere (after "What is the meaning of life?" and "Who was that lady I saw you with last night?")—should be an incidental but nevertheless Number One concern for anybody purporting to write a definitive account of what is known about the strangest stop (if one may be permitted a metaphor) on the Bach family organ.

One of the answers to the question is tied to the development of the long-playing record: the over-idolizing of historical figures is usually followed by a period of debunking, and during the last couple of decades, which have seen the recording of virtually everything written by J. S. Bach, there has naturally developed an interest in the soft underbelly of eighteenth-century music, the so-called Seamy Side of the Baroque. This is perfectly normal and nothing to be worried about.

For another answer to the question we may adopt the reasoning of a United States senator from the midwest, who, when one of then-President Nixon's nominees to the Supreme Court was criticized as being "mediocre," came to the nominee's defense by pointing out that many people in this country are mediocre, and why shouldn't they be represented on the Supreme Court? The author has actually found that P. D. Q. Bach's music is capable of having a therapeutic effect on audiences; the works of J. S. Bach and Mozart are so serenely perfect that many people come away from hearing them with an aggravated inferiority complex caused by the knowledge that no matter how hard they try they can never hope to achieve such beauty, whereas hearing the works of P. D. Q. Bach comforts the listener with the ego-building and not unrealistic feeling that, even if he has had no music lessons, he could easily do as well with one ear, as it were, tied behind his back.

Finally, the author has been the victim of many attacks, ranging from the petty to the downright dangerous, by various vested interests as well as parties in two-piece suits; the nature of some of these assaults is touched upon in the pages that follow, but one of the charges, the vilest, most scurrilously scandalous of them all, must be mentioned here: the insinuation, sometimes made subtly and sometimes blatantly, that P. D. Q. Bach is a figmental entity, a being no less the creation of this author than was Tarzan of Edgar Rice Burroughs or Howard Hughes of Clifford Irving. It should be unnecessary for a tenured university professor to defend himself against such a patently false accusation, such an absurd calumny, such a big fat lie, but under the circumstances he must welcome the opportunity provided in these pages to present the evidence and, it is hoped, silence forever the seemingly numberless Doubting Thomases, Richards, and Harolds who (to our eternal shame) fill most of our musical chairs.

P.S.

University of Southern North Dakota at Hoople
23 July 1975
11:47 p.m.

Preface to the English Language Edition

It may seem, on first thought, somewhat redundant to include a "Preface to the English Language Edition" in a book that was written in the English language in the first place and has not even been translated into any other languages anyway. But if the reader will bear with him for a moment the author would like to point out that if P. D. Q. Bach had not been effectively elbowed out of the bus of history for nearly two centuries, scholarly inquiry into his life and work would have begun in its proper place, that is to say, Germany and Austria, and there would by now have been, if not an entire book, at least several articles in the various German-language musicological journals. With this in mind, and in order partly to make up for this lack, the author has tried to preserve the lengthy sentences and fastidious punctuation that would have characterized those articles had they been written.

P.S.

University of Southern North Dakota at Hoople
24 July 1975
12:03 a.m.

Foreword

"Know thyself," said Romeo to Portia, and he might have added, "Know thy audience." Perhaps the most important decision the author of a scholarly work must make is: For whom is this book written? Is it written for the author's fellow scholars, for (in this case) musicians in general, or for that broad, undifferentiated mass known as the lay public?

The experience of the past decade and a half has shown that interest—whether it takes the form of attraction or repulsion—in P. D. Q. Bach can be found in all three of the above-mentioned categories. For this reason the author of the present work has attempted to meld several different stylistic approaches into one verbal salad, so to speak, combining the exhaustive attention to detail found in scholarly writing with the anecdotal appeal of the more "popular" biography. Many of P. D. Q. Bach's most ardent admirers are not yet able to read, and they will be pleased to discover that the book is profusely illustrated, whereas the trained musician will find food for thought in the technical analysis of a P. D. Q. Bach piece which constitutes one of the appendices.

It is to be hoped that when this humble literary effort takes its final bow in the eyes of its beholders it will be found to have had, as the saying goes, something for everyone and everyone for something.

Introduction

The most controversial aspect of P. D. Q. Bach's life, aside from its existence, is the time of its existence, that is, his dates. It has become traditional to list his dates as they were inscribed on his first tomb: 1807–1742; this has led to a great deal of confusion and a seemingly endless flow of possible explanations.

Various theories based on the assumption that he was born in 1807 and died in 1742 are too fanciful to merit serious consideration, which, however, has not kept them from receiving wide dissemination and even acceptance. More plausible is the idea that the inscription was a comment on P. D. Q.'s artistic development; no one who has studied the complete *corpus* of his surviving works will disagree with the statement that his most individual pieces were written at the beginning of his composing career (he was thirty-five years old before he began composing, writing the works that were to catapult him into obscurity) after which he proceeded, throughout the dregs of his days, to forget everything he knew, writing music that more and more resembled the music he had heard as a child. But in the light of the rest of his family's attitude toward P. D. Q., fully documented in the following pages, there is no doubt in the author's mind that the inscription was simply a clumsy and transparent attempt on the part of certain influential members of the Bach family to make it appear that P. D. Q. could not possibly have been sired by Johann Sebastian, who died in 1750.

Since however, there is no documentary evidence supporting one or another of these or any other explanations, the author always includes a question mark with the dates: (1807–1742)?, in the belief that discretion is nine-tenths, or at least the better part of, the law.

Author's Note

E♭, although early in the morning
it is sometimes as low as C♯ or even C.

Acknowledgments

A project of this scope could not be realized without the aid of many people, or rather it *could,* but it would be dumb to do it that way when there are so many people around willing to give their aid. It is impossible to thank by name every single person who helped, and many married people must also remain anonymous, but it would be a crying shame if the author didn't mention those to whom he is most deeply indebted, no matter how tedious the list may become.

Stephen Schmidt's strange inability to foresee the consequences of his actions enabled him to suggest that the author perform the music of P. D. Q. Bach, not just within the bounds of the university community, but for the general public at large; his contributions as a producer, manager, friend and co-conspirator have been immeasurably immense and have extended into every aspect of the public exposure (so important in this post-Watergate era!) of P. D. Q. Bach: concerts, records, published music, television, and this book.

Hardly less important have been the contributions of William "Bill" Walters. Hired originally as a stage manager, he has within the space of less than a decade become much more: staunch ally, canny cohort, patient friend, and without a doubt the second most knowledgeable authority on P. D. Q. Bach in the world; in fact he has occasionally caught the author in an embarrassing slip of the memory or tongue. In addition to providing helpful ideas and constant criticism, he has been responsible for restoring and rebuilding many of the unique instruments for which P. D. Q. wrote; all of his work in this area is incomparable, but his masterpiece must surely be the chamber caliope used by the author in performances of the *Toot Suite*.

The research involved in putting together the visual material for this book and the slide-lecture presentation which is part of *The Intimate P. D. Q. Bach* concert is staggering, which cannot be said of Joan Abrahams, who has never once been seen "under the influence" by the author during the entire four years of their often intense working relationship. As a graduate student in the seminar on "Originality Through Incompetence" she participated in several important "digs," but her cheerful energy and unflagging disposition have fully justified her promotion to the job of Researcher.

Gratitude must also be expressed for the patience of Charlotte Mayerson, the Random House editor who ended eight years of procrastination on the part of the author without ever raising her voice.

Several fine photographers are represented in these pages; their names are listed in alphabetical order, starting with the earliest letter of the alphabet that begins a last name: Paul Buck Hoeffler, Kim Massie, Norman Vershay, and William Walters (modesty prevents the author from including his own name in the list). Special mention must be made of Jim Kalett for his exceptionally lifelike copy photography of most of the graphic material in the book.

Restoring an old painting, especially under the circumstances surrounding the discovery of the "official" portrait of P. D. Q. Bach, is a ticklish proposition, and Mara McAfee is to be commended for her stunning success with an unusually difficult problem.

Many members of the author's seminars at the U. of S.N.D. at H. have contributed to P. D. Q. Bach research, but some must be mentioned. Lawrence Widdoes deserves much more credit than any grade the author could give him for his role in discovering the manuscript fragments, attempts at engraving, sketches, etc., that are found at the end of Part III. Most of this material was unearthed single-handedly by Mr. Widdoes. Cathy Aison was of inestimable value in restoring the documents pertaining to P. D. Q. and in producing the maps in Appendices A and B. Graham Blackburn realized the Bach family tree in Appendix H, Mel Klapholz and Jules Maidoff unearthed drawings, while Diane Lampert found the portraits of Porcelina Speck and Prince Fred. Other students not yet mentioned who have participated on field trips are James Burr, Kay and John Keffer, Tony Santaniello and Mary Jo Walters; they're all good kids, and whether or not they continue in musicology, they'll make fine citizens. Joseph Abrahams, Mrs. Farrell, and Russell Ryan were especially helpful in tracking down P. D. Q. Bach's descendants, and Gerda Lerner provided the translation of P. D. Q.'s original epitaph.

One of the author's earliest associates was his brother David, who helped define the three creative periods of P. D. Q.'s life and establish some of the first-known biographical details. He also wrote the liner notes for the first phonograph album when all other scholars refused to have anything to do with it.

Vanguard Records is to be praised for its courage in continuing to record the music of P. D. Q. Bach, and even to release it, as is the Theodore Presser Co. for continuing to publish it, although with the information the author has on Maynard and Seymour Solomon at the former concern and Arnold Broido at the latter, they really have very little choice.

The list goes on and on. Harold Shaw, who had the perfect opportunity to "drop" P. D. Q. Bach when he left the Hurok organization to form his own booking agency, figured what the hell, for which we must all be grateful. George Schutz and Gary Haber have given out handbills on the street when holier-than-thou conservatory students have refused to help advertise the annual concerts of P. D. Q.'s music in New York City. Robert Lasky continues to handle the sometimes sticky legal matters in spite of threats of disbarment.

Gary Farmer and Suzanne Boorsch at the Department of Prints and Photographs of the Metropolitan Museum have been more than helpful, whatever that means, as have the staff of the New York Public Library. Pat Diffley and her staff at Suite 1006 brightened the day during the author's most monastic period of work, and Doug Kenney —enough of this! Who *cares* about Doug Kenney? The author doesn't know about you, but the author can't take many more of these cotton-pickin' *names!* Jorge Mester, John Ferrante, Maurice Eisenstadt, John Nelson, Robert Dennis, Stanley Walden, Vincent Persichetti, Sigvald and Isabelle Thompson, Ernest Lloyd, my wife, my mother and father, my uncle, my step-grandmother who lives in Ames, Iowa. There, that's it! The author thanks you all, now let's get on with it.

Table of Contents

I

P. D. Q. BACH'S BACKGROUND: CAUSE OR EFFECT?

"... the Graces, too,
with girdles all unloosed ..."
—Horace, Odes

EARLY INFANCY
(1742-1745)

IT[1] was cold and dark and wet in Leipzig on the night of the 31st of March 1742. The darkness was not unexpected, but the extreme cold was without precedent, and it had been raining incessantly for three weeks, as if in preparation for some dire event.

In the home of the Cantor of St. Thomas' Church, however, it was warm and light and dry, due to the large sheaf of Vivaldi manuscripts burning in the fireplace.[2]

At fifty-seven, Johann Sebastian Bach was at the height of his creative powers, a position he had maintained for over fifty years, ever since he started composing small works for the organ at Lüneburg.[3]

One can imagine him working feverishly on part IV of his *Clavierübung*[4] with nothing but a few concerti grossi for light, only dimly aware, at the height as he was of his creative powers, that in the adjoining room his second wife was giving birth to his twenty-first child. Since there was obviously very little novelty in the situation, Bach probably barely looked up when the midwife announced that "something has been born";[5] upon seeing the child, however, the master's initial indifference gave way to a feeling of benign antipathy, a feeling which remained constant for the eight years of life that were left to him. At the age of five, the boy still had not been given a name, and it was only after repeated exhortations by his eldest brother, Wilhelm Friedemann, that his father bestowed upon him, not a name, but—at least—three initials: P. D. Q. When Wilhelm Friedemann asked what the initials stood for, his father said they stood for nothing, which indeed could be said of P. D. Q. himself later in his life. Old Johann Sebastian added something about using up all the available names on his first twenty children, and years later P. D. Q. Bach wrote to a friend, "In all truthfulness I can say that to this day I have no idea as to what, if anything, my name represents." In the same letter he attributed his frequent headaches to the fact that he had been christened in a shipyard rather than in a church.

And so it was that on that cold, dark, wet night in Leipzig (at one minute after midnight, to be precise), there came into this world one of the most curious figures in the entire history of music in

---

[1] i.e., the weather, according to the unique diary kept throughout his entire life by the Margrave Bernhard Erich von Brandigburg (1738-1743); in it he recorded in minute detail each day's weather conditions, and nothing else. It was published in forty-three volumes by Schlaff of Düsterburg in 1762, but by then the weather of Bernhard Erich's time was considered dull and old-fashioned, and consequently it aroused little interest until the 1840's, when Felix Memmessohn's enormously popular "Baroque Weather Reports" started a renaissance of early weather research which has continued unabated to the present day.

[2] Johann Sebastian Bach, whenever he came into possession of a manuscript by another composer, used to make his own arrangement of the work and then burn the original, thus cornering the market. Fortunately, his arrangements were better than the original works—or were they?

[3] "Small Work No. 1 for the Organ," Bach's first composition, has been lost.

[4] Keyboard Übung.

[5] This unfortunate phrase was overheard by the new arrival, and it rankled him for the rest of his life.

Western Civilization; a man who did not change the course of music one iota, a man who defined definitively the doctrine of originality through incompetence, a man who triumphed over the most staggering obstacle ever placed before a composer: absolute and utter lack of talent. In the years that followed, P. D. Q. Bach steadfastly ignored handicaps that would have sent other men into teaching or government, resulting in a body of works that is without parallel.[1]

Many great composers were ignored during their own lifetime, but P. D. Q. stands out as a monument to ignorance. Not only was he ignored at a very early age, as we have already seen, but one might even say that he was prenatally ignored, since Anna Magdalena Bach had given away all her maternity clothes after her thirteenth (J. S. Bach's twentieth) child was born.[2] Thus exposed to the wind and sun during the day, and to the low temperatures, lack of light, and dampness of the cold, dark, wet Leipzig nights, the young lad (or "boy," as his father called him) soon developed a thick skin which was to serve him well in later years. But although he was ignored, he was not mistreated, and he seems to have had a pleasant childhood, spending most of his time doing all the florid little things that Baroque children did. He was too young to be doing any copying for his father, he was even too young to be pumping the bellows of the church organ (although he did occasionally crawl under the keyboard while his father was playing and sit on one of the pedals; the resulting musical effect is known as a pedal point, and throughout his life

P. D. Q. expressed his preference for pedal point over counterpoint and even needlepoint), so he simply played games and ran away from home a few times.[3]

If we attempt to find the seeds of P. D. Q. Bach's personality as a composer in the events of these first three formative years, we will be hard put indeed to do so. In the first place, information on this period is very spotty, since it consists entirely of entries in Johanna Carolina Bach's leopard-skin diary; in the second place, there was virtually nothing, since most of the family records were lost when they moved from the first place.

P. D. Q. Bach was the last, and by all means the least, of Johann Sebastian Bach's twenty-odd children, and he was certainly the oddest of the lot. So much so, in fact, that we are tempted to wonder whether old J. S. really *was* still at the height of his creative powers, until we remember that in the life of an artistic giant the spirit can function quite distinctly from the flesh; the towering genius that was Bach had already sired a ne'er-do-well, Johann Gottfried Bernhard, whose principle activity in life was getting into debt and letting his father bail him out, and also an idiot son, Gottfried Heinrich; Wilhelm Friedemann reputedly drank to excess, and according to one source Christian Gottlieb was mixed up in dealings of dubious legality with members of the underworld.[4] Thus we see that P. D. Q., possessing as he did a combination of many of the traits of previous Bach children, can in a sense be

---

[1] historically speaking, that is. Musically the body of works contains many parallels, especially fifths and octaves.

[2] One can hardly blame her.

[3] "Walked away from home" would be more accurate. P. D. Q.'s laziness manifested itself right from the beginning; as a tiny baby he discovered that even crying took more effort than it was worth, except during concerts and services.

[4] The fact that C. G. died at the age of three, however, casts a shadow of suspicion on this accusation.

regarded as a summation of Bach the father, just as *The Art of the Fugue* is a summation of Bach the composer. In addition to the characteristics mentioned above, P. D. Q. possessed the originality of Johann Christian, the arrogance of Carl Philipp Emanuel, and the obscurity of Johann Christoph Friedrich.

P. D. Q.'s early infancy ended with a striking decision; at the age of three, P. D. Q. Bach decided to give up music.

2
LATE INFANCY
(1745-1766)

THE decision, as important as it was, went largely unnoticed in the Bach family, due probably to the fact that up until that point the boy had shown no interest in music whatsoever. Another reason it went unnoticed is that P. D. Q. didn't tell anyone about it, since he had not yet learned how to talk. But forty years later he still remembered it well when he wrote to a friend from Wein-am-Rhein:

Sometimes when I am sober I wish that I had held firm to the resolve I made at the age of three, namely, to give up music for the rest of my life. Whether the feeling of melancholy that descends upon me at those times is due to the lack of a spirit of satisfaction in my life, or simply to the lack of those more easily obtainable spirits, I cannot say, but I have found that apply-

ing a remedy to the second of the two possible causes seems to remedy the first as well, with the result that such periods are happily few and far between.

Exactly why he made the decision at this time we can only surmise, but the most likely explanation is that it was a gesture of defiance to his father. For the reasons outlined above, it seems improbable that the fateful decision had any effect on Johann Sebastian Bach; although, two years later, he did finally allow the boy to be christened, he also paid his son the ultimate gesture of indifference, in 1750, by dying. This is a traumatic experience for any eight-year-old boy, no matter what his feelings toward his father are, and P. D. Q. Bach's *Traumarei*, written when the composer was in his thirties, shows that he had not yet learned how to write for the piano.

After Big Daddy Bach (as he was never called) died, his family gradually dispersed; he left no will, so his estate was divided among his survivors, one-third going to Anna Magdalena, and the rest, including five claviers, two lute-harpsichords, and ten string instruments, being split up among the children.[1] P. D. Q., characteristically enough, was left with virtually nothing: his share of Bach's legacy was one kazoo.[2] The idiot son was taken over by one of the daughters, who was married; young Johann Christian was taken to Berlin by Carl Philipp Emanuel; Anna Magdalena ended up in a poorhouse; what happened to P. D. Q.? Here the Bach family's two-century-old conspiracy of silence has been most effective. Whether someone in the

---

[1] rendering the instruments, of course, unplayable.
[2] See page 227.

family took him, or whether at the age of eight, he had to strike out on his own, is not recorded.[1] There was only one orphanage in Leipzig at the time, run by a certain Carl Orph, who kept careful records on all the children in his custody, and P. D. Q. Bach's name does not appear. One suspects that he was left to his own devices, since the next reference we have indicates that he tried unsuccessfully to join the Imperial Infantry, which, in spite of its name, did not take children.

By 1755, he was in Dudeldorf, apprenticed to a man named Ludwig Zahnstocher, who had discovered the trick of playing melodies on the saw, using a violin bow. The "musical saw," as it is now called,[2] was a tremendous success; accompanied by P. D. Q. at the clavier, Zahnstocher played jigs and other lively dances to astonished audiences whose members implored him to explain how it was done, leading finally to an article in the local press entitled THE JIG-SAW PUZZLE SOLVED. With the publication of this article, Zahnstocher lost his monopoly, and after an unsuccessful attempt to make his living as a virtuoso, went back to carpentry. He wrote to his son, Kleiner, who was a violinist in the Mannheim Orchestra:

I have decided to go back into woodworking, what with my fortunes in the music business being at such a low ebb. You will laugh at me and point out how many violinists there are, and say you still make a good living there in Mannheim. But somehow it is different with the saw. In the first place it hasn't been accepted into the orchestras, even though it is cer-

[1] See Schwann, *Long-Playing Record Catalogue*, March 1975.
[2] Zahnstocher, who could play in one key only, called it the "C-saw."

tainly more uplifting to listen to than the oafish hunting horns, for which they are even writing concertos nowadays! Secondly, there are so many amateur sawists around now that hardly anybody comes to my concerts any more. Besides, my accompanist (whose father, by the way, was the great organist Sebastian Bach) says he wants to get out of music anyway, and I've persuaded him to continue as my apprentice at the shop. I'm sending your bow back to you in a separate package—has anyone noticed that you've been playing your violin with an umbrella?

P. D. Q., by now a teenager, did indeed continue to serve Zahnstocher as an apprentice carpenter, and in addition to the profitable activity of turning out prefabricated water closets (their most refined model, the Claude Achille W.C., was quite popular among the nobility), the two craftsmen-musicians, so different in age and character, collaborated on a series of investigations and experiments which are without equal in the history of music or carpentry.

Their first project was an attempt to fashion a set of locks for all the major and minor keys, an endeavor as hopeless as it was pointless, and which was abandoned in favor of a more practical idea: the mechanical finger-conditioner and self-practicer. This ingenious device consisted of a pair of wooden gloves equipped with elaborate spring mechanisms which controlled each finger independently. If a harpsichordist wished to limber up his fingers and relax his hands, he would merely wind up the springs and place his hands in the gloves, which would bend and unbend his fingers with a gentle massaging motion. By far the more interesting use, however, of the Zahnstocher mechanical glove was as a self-practicer. By programming, as we would say now, a difficult passage in a piece of keyboard music on two strips of paper not unlike player piano rolls, and inserting the strips into slots in the gloves, the harpsichordist could not only watch and listen as the gloves played the passage on the keyboard, but also, by inserting his hands in the gloves as they played, he could actually experience what it felt like to be playing the passage properly; in other words, the gloves were literally doing his practicing for him, conditioning, in the Pavlovian sense,[1] his fingers to perform correctly. The mechanical gloves raised great hopes in the hearts of their inventors, who even started working on a vastly more complex model for organists, involving foot-gloves, or as they are even more confusingly called in German, foot-hand-shoes *(Fusshandschuhe)* for practicing the pedals.

Unfortunately, a tragic incident occurred which undermined the whole project. Prince Ferdinand the Insignificant, a member of the lesser nobility, expressed an interest in the self-practicer and even visited Zahnstocher's shop in person to try it out. He arrived one afternoon, unannounced, just as P. D. Q. was attaching an optional accessory which they had thought of adding for those who could afford it: an automatic fingernail cutter which did its work while the owner practiced. Of course, it was a mistake to allow the Prince to try out the new model before testing it themselves, but Zahnstocher and P. D. Q. were undoubtedly so busy thinking up ever more extravagant compliments with which to ingratiate themselves in the eyes of

their esteemed visitor, that they completely neglected those common rules of safety of which they were probably only dimly aware anyway. To dwell upon sensational details would be to violate the scholarly nature of the present work; suffice it therefore to say that Ferd the Four-Fingered, as he came to be called, died of natural causes before he could wreak revenge.

The last project on which P. D. Q. worked with Zahnstocher began through curious coincidence. After the Prince's disastrous visit, an immediate departure to some other part of the country seemed advisable, and the sooner the better; within a matter of minutes the hapless inventors had left Dudeldorf and were on their way to Baden-Baden-Baden, a charming spa in southern Germany conveniently close to the Swiss border. Ferdinand, in his blind rage, had left his purse behind, and since meeting him again would almost certainly have meant forfeiting their lives, Zahnstocher and his apprentice decided to try and make do with what they had, which included Ferdinand's purse. This made their stay in Baden-Baden-Baden particularly enjoyable, and it was while taking the waters one brisk autumn morning that they made the acquaintance of one Johann Gottlieb Goldberg. It turned out that he, Goldberg, had been harpsichordist to Count von Kayserling, the Russian ambassador to the court at Dresden, and the man for whom Johann Sebastian Bach had written one of his greatest pieces, to be played during the Count's frequent attacks of insomnia; in short, this was the Goldberg of the *"Goldberg" Variations!* Upon learning this, in spite of his less-than-warm feelings toward his father, it was all young P. D. Q. Bach could do to hold back a flood of nostalgic tears, for

---

[1] Not that his fingers salivated, of course, but rather that they learned new tricks.

the *"Goldberg" Variations* had been published the year that P. D. Q. was born, and the last variation of the set quoted two folk songs that the family used to sing, and which he even remembered singing himself once in a while to empty out the house.

It is tempting to speculate about the thoughts that must have crossed P. D. Q.'s mind as he lay on his back, floating in the warm mineral waters. It was now five years since he had left home. Where was his mother? And his brothers and sisters? Were there still Bach family gatherings? Could Wilhelm Friedemann hold his liquor any better?

His mind must have been as flooded with thoughts as was his nose with water, for he had fallen asleep, and probably would have drowned had Goldberg not noticed his peruke floating on the surface. "We had to fish my apprentice out of the water today," Zahnstocher wrote to his son; "I've never known such a lazy person—he knows how to float, but not how to swim! I think he would be quite content just to float downstream all his life, taking everything as it comes, never making any effort to go against the current." The next sentence in this letter is particularly interesting; it shows how P. D. Q. was constantly hounded by his family's reputation, and yet how independent of his family's thinking he had already become. "He'll never live up to his name with that kind of an attitude," Zahnstocher continues, "but I like him anyway—he's good company, and he's always willing to try out a new idea, no matter how extraordinary it seems, which is more than you could say for his illustrious father."

During the course of their conversations Goldberg mentioned that his new employer, the Archduke von Trio, was the exact opposite of Count von Kayserling; that is, he slept so soundly that nothing in the world seemed to be able to waken him. He slept so deeply and so long that doctors frequently decided that he was in a coma and called for a priest, but he always awoke in fine health, his only concern being the fear that he had slept through something important, such as a war. When Goldberg said that the Archduke had posted a reward to be paid to anyone who could produce a sound which would rouse him from his slumbers when necessary, Zahnstocher and P. D. Q. lost no time waiting around. The news of Prince Ferdinand's death had reached Baden-Baden-Baden, which meant that it was safe to return to Dudeldorf, and by the very next morning the two ex-fugitives had packed their purse and set off for home. Immediately upon their return, they started designing what may have been the loudest instrument ever created: the Pandemonium.[1]

In the midst of finishing and mastering "Thor's music box," as Zahnstocher liked to call the Pandemonium, P. D. Q., suddenly and without warning, packed his bags and vanished from sight. Taken completely by surprise, Zahnstocher professed total ignorance as to the motives for the departure of his apprentice, although we may surmise that it had something to do with the impending presentation of the Pandemonium to the Archduke. P. D. Q. had on numerous occasions expressed concern over the possible side effects of the sound of the instrument, and it is probably no coincidence that he left the day after he learned that the name of the Archduke's alpine palace was Das Glaslusthaus (The Pavilion of Glass). Zahnstocher went ahead

---

[1] A diagram of the Pandemonium appears on page 53.

with his plans, but exactly what happened at the final presentation we can only guess, since his letters to his son stop abruptly on the afternoon of his arrival at the palace. Suffice it to say that the fact that the largest avalanche in European history occurred on the following day seems peculiarly relevant.

It is with a real sense of regret that we come to the end of this remarkable collaboration, because Zahnstocher's letters provide us with the only day-to-day documentation of P. D. Q. Bach's life that we have, and they cover such a short period of time.[1] Also, it is refreshing to have come across someone who was willing to take P. D. Q. in spite of face value, and it is perhaps this quality of sympathy (or was it empathy?) that makes Zahnstocher seem so sympathetic, or empathetic.[2] He was a man of great curiosity and a certain crude wit which, together with his infectious enthusiasm, must have made him an obnoxious man to be with;[3] and yet P. D. Q. always spoke fondly of him in later life, and it is easy to see why.

[1] His son published the letters in 1781, but being something of a social climber, he "translated" them from Very Low German[i] into Old Middle Fairly High German; fortunately the author of the present work was able to locate the original letters before they were destroyed. He found them in the backyard incinerator of Luke Zahnstocher, of Zap, North Dakota, who would already have burned them had it not been raining for ten days, which is very unusual in Zap.

[i] Not to be confused with Gutteral German, which P. D. Q. himself spoke later in his life, if not at this point; Gutteral German is a form of Very Low German which is distinguished by its halting speech pattern, characteristic of those who lie in gutters.

[2] or simply pathetic.

[3] After the Prince Ferdinand incident Zahnstocher is said to have mused, "Here's a paradox: if one has no forefinger, one has four fingers," but since this is even less a paradox in German than it is in English, the story is probably apocryphal.

At the end of January 1756, P. D. Q. showed up in Salzburg, carrying with him a letter of introduction to the first violinist and leader of the court orchestra, Leopold Mozart. The significance of this letter, it goes without saying, cannot be underestimated, for it led to the historic meeting between P. D. Q., approaching his fourteenth birthday, and Wolfgang Amadeus Mozart, already three days old and just beginning to talk. P. D. Q. immediately sensed a great talent in the lad, and recommended to his father that he be given rigorous training from an early age, saying that if this were done the boy would undoubtedly become one of the greatest billiards players of all time. Apparently Leopold did not take seriously the advice of his visitor, who was, after all, some twenty-three years his junior, as well as his visitor, for, as is well known, he, Leopold, allowed his son to dabble in music, willy-nilly, to the virtual exclusion of billiards, and yet, later in his, Wolfgang's, life, in spite, as it were, of this neglect, he, Wolfgang, owned his own billiards table, and loved nothing, by his own admission, better than to play a game with his friends, all the while writing out his latest symphony, or, if such were the case, quartet, or whatever.

Although he apparently liked Salzburg,[4] P. D. Q. did not stay around long; within a few months he realized that the Mozart boy was already beginning to outshine him as a musician, and he lost no time in leaving for browner pastures. After all, he had spent the first eight years of his life (and what important years those are!) surrounded by musical genius, and the experience was one he was not anxious to repeat. He had undoubtedly heard the

[4] Years later he told a friend, "I apparently liked Salzburg."

expression "It is better to be a big fish in a small pond than a small fish in a big pond," and the first thirty-five years of P. D. Q. Bach's life can be looked upon as being a search for the proper pond, a puddle tiny enough to make him, by comparison, a big fish. Surprisingly enough, he was eventually successful in this search, but a discussion of Wein-am-Rhein would be decidedly out of place at this point, and must be left to a later chapter.

After Salzburg we must trace P. D. Q.'s footsteps as best we can, with little more than fleeting references to guide us. Already at fourteen a seasoned traveler and a remarkably independent and self-sufficient young man, he wandered around Europe, floating in and out of various towns, schools, and jobs. His name appears on a 1757 list of pupils at the Aufimmer Hochschule für Castrati in Muhen-bad, a famous academy for the training of young men who had been persuaded, by means of surgery, to remain sopranos for the rest of their lives. P. D. Q.'s career at Forever High was short-lived, however, since he had not had the requisite anatomical modification, and was therefore an impostor; a note attached to the enrollment list explains that when Farinelli, probably the greatest castrato singer of the day, visited the school and heard the choir perform, he immediately singled out P. D. Q. and exposed him. The lad was promptly expelled, undoubtedly losing face, but otherwise intact.

Sometime within the next five years he went to Dublin, where he visited a distant cousin who was an artist and writer as well as a musician, Schwein-hard Bach. It was no doubt P. D. Q.'s intention to convince his cousin to take him on as an apprentice, or at least to put him up for a while, but Schweinhard (or "Piggy," as he was called by all who knew him), had too many problems of his own to put up with "a scruffy little ruffian whose ears are as large as they are untutored, and whose idea of virtuosity is to play the harpsichord with his feet, completely disregarding the rules of fingering and phrasing, not to mention those of common decency."[1] The Dublin Bach had written an opera to his own libretto, *Die Freuden Jakobs*,[2] which created an enormous scandal when it was performed; officials of both the town council and the Church described it as "tending to stir the sex impulses or to lead to sexually impure and lustful thoughts." Defenders of the opera replied that while its effect on the audience "undoubtedly is somewhat emetic, nowhere does it tend to be an aphrodisiac." Since opportunities to see a dirty opera were very rare outside of royal circles, even those Dubliners who supported the town council and Church made sure that they saw it at least two or three times "in order to corroborate first impressions, thus precluding the possibility of unjust censure founded upon hastily formed opinions." The forces of righteousness eventually won out by setting fire to the theater, but by then Piggy had made

---

[1] The letter from which this is quoted was written to Tobias Friedrich Bach, another cousin of P. D. Q., and is extremely significant, for it goes on to say, "One cannot but doubt that this juvenile delinquent is indeed a *true and full* member of the Bach family." [emphasis added—PS] It was probably this letter that started the rumor, still current among descendants of the Bach family, that P. D. Q. was an illegitimate child. Although there is absolutely no foundation of truth for this accusation, the alacrity of its dissemination and acceptance throughout the family is not surprising, since, if true, it would relieve the family of at least some of the responsibility for having produced a composer whom his brother Johann Christian called "a pimple on the face of music."

[2] *James's Joys.*

enough money to purchase a dukedom in Italy; here he spent the rest of his life enjoying the prerogatives of nobility and producing a series of etchings which were recently rediscovered when the library of former King Farouk was confiscated.

Although Piggy Bach refused to have anything to do with P. D. Q. Bach, the similarities between the two relatives are more striking than their differences. "Emetic" is a word that was often used to describe P. D. Q.'s music, and the titles of several P. D. Q. Bach works, such as *Serenude* and *Pervertimento,* indicate that the extramusical interests of their composer were not entirely dissimilar to those of his Dublin kinsman.[1] Both Bachs were renegades, although Piggy tried, and to a certain extent managed, to maintain good relations with the rest of his family (like Johann Christian, however, he converted to Catholicism, and it is no accident that when he chose a place to spend the rest of his life he chose not Germany, but Italy.)[2] Also, Piggy was notoriously lazy, using labor-saving devices very similar to those employed years later by P. D. Q. Finally, Piggy loved eating and drinking, as he once said, "Even better than art, in fact there's no comparison."[3] Whether at the time of their meeting

this was a similarity to, or an influence upon P. D. Q., is hard to say, but by 1780, the aesthetic outlook of the two men was virtually identical.

Sometime after leaving Dublin, P. D. Q. went to London to visit his brother Johann Christian Bach. One would have thought that the two brothers would be quite close,[4] since they were the last two sons born to Johann Sebastian Bach, but judging by the doodle on one of P. D. Q.'s sketchbook pages showing his brother hanging from a gallows,[5] P. D. Q. felt even more animosity toward J. C. than he did toward J. S. and C. P. E., not to mention J. C. F.[6] It was Johann Christian who coined the term "noisemonger" to describe his younger brother, and although he allowed P. D. Q. (for a price) to stay in his house, he insisted that "the kid" always use the servants' entrance.

Aside from a few scattered facts, we know precious little about P. D. Q.'s visit to London. In fact, we lose sight of him completely until he turns up at the home of Leonhard Sigismund Dietrich Bach, who, situated as he was in St. Petersburg, was probably P. D. Q.'s most distant cousin. L. S. D. Bach had just returned from a trip to America, one of the highlights of which was a demonstration of the Glass Harmonica by its inventor, Benjamin Franklin. It is well known that a tone may be obtained by running a wet finger around the rim of a drinking glass; Franklin harnessed this phenomenon

---

[1] In making this comparison, of course, we are looking ahead, musically at least, to the P. D. Q. Bach of the 1780's; the P. D. Q. Bach of the 1760's had not yet started composing.

[2] Upon the death of Pope Clement XIV in 1769 he traveled to Rome and tried to start a write-in campaign among the College of Cardinals, planning to call himself Pope Alexander, after his idol, Alexander Pope. The cardinals, however, were offended by the BACH FOR POPE buttons and T-shirts he sent them, and when he pasted "Let's put Bach in the Basilica" posters all over the Piazza San Pietro they issued a joint bill entitled "Mirabilis facta est hutzpa tua" ("Thy hutzpah is become wonderful") ordering him out of Rome.

[3] He later amplified this statement, saying, "That's the trouble with art: you can't drink it."

[4] although not as close as P. D. Q. and Regine Susanna, who were born about a month apart.

[5] which is reproduced on page 146, and dates, of course, from much later in his life.

[6] which nobody ever does.

for musical use by developing a mechanism that kept the rims of a mounted set of glasses wet, and the instrument enjoyed a great popularity in Europe, with Mozart, Beethoven, and Padre Martini numbered among the many composers who wrote music for it. When P. D. Q. came on the scene, Leonhard had just finished building his own model and was experimenting with an original idea which he was sure would improve the tone quality: using wine instead of water to wet the glasses. He finally admitted that there was no audible difference, but not until after he and P. D. Q. had tried out fifty-seven wines of various locales and vintages. Quite apart from the fact that it was rather expensive, using wine had the additional disadvantage of tempting the player to lick his fingers frequently, a motion unnecessary to the operation of the instrument and usually done at the sacrifice of several notes.

P. D. Q. must have been pleasantly surprised by the friendliness of his reception in St. Petersburg, but when Leonhard sobered up he became considerably less amiable,[1] and the final straw was a development that affords us a rare glimpse into P. D. Q.'s amorous history. Leonhard had a daughter, Betty-Sue, who had not quite turned fourteen, and P. D. Q. was given the task of instructing her on the piano. Apparently, however, the instruction took place under the piano as well as on it, and when Betty-Sue started exhibiting symptoms of morning sickness, her father started looking for his shotgun, which weapon, however, he did not find in time to prevent P. D. Q. from achieving one of

the hastiest departures of a life filled with hasty departures.

After St. Petersburg, P. D. Q. never again made any attempt to seek help from, or even to establish contact with, his family, much to the relief of the latter, whose feelings about seeing him were candidly expressed by another cousin, Peter Ulrich Bach;[2] In 1755, Peter Ulrich wrote to Carl Philipp Emanuel: "Like the effects of certain diseases, P. D. Q. appears periodically, causing increasingly acute discomfort with each visit."

It has undoubtedly become apparent to even the most casual reader that the vow of musical abstinence which he made at the age of three had by no means been strictly observed by P. D. Q. up to this point; yet it is also obvious from some of Zahnstocher's remarks that P. D. Q. had by no means forgotten the vow altogether. Although he tried time and time again to extract himself from all musical endeavor, he could no more resist the siren song of St. Cecelia than he could resist dropping in on his relatives in spite of their open hostility. There is, of course, an intimate connection between the two things against which he was struggling; since during the seventeenth and eighteenth centuries the name Bach was synonymous with music, P. D. Q.'s ambiguous feelings toward his family were naturally accompanied by ambiguous feelings toward their art. And yet it was perhaps this very conflict that imparted to P. D. Q.'s early

---

[1] a fact which made a deep impression on P. D. Q.

[2] Since he lived in Mausendorf, only a few miles from Dudeldorf, P. U. probably had more contact with P. D. Q. than most members of the family.

years the fund of energy, so conspicuously absent during his maturity, that enabled him to overcome his fundamentally slothlike nature at least to a certain extent: after all, he worked with Zahnstocher and traveled all over Europe, when he could easily have been vegetating in a poorhouse. For as Jung has said:

Just as all energy proceeds from opposition, so the psyche too possesses its inner polarity, this being the indispensable prerequisite for its aliveness, as Heraclitus realized long ago. Both theoretically and practically, polarity is inherent in all living things. Set against this overpowering force is the fragile unity of the ego, which has come into being in the course of millennia only with the aid of countless protective measures.[1]

Following this line of thought leads us to the realization that in the 1760's the unity of the ego was two centuries younger than it is now; that is, it was lacking two hundred years' worth of protective measures compared to the unity of Jung's ego, itself described as being in fragile condition. So it should come as no surprise that P. D. Q. Bach was having trouble with the unity of *his* ego, and that after more than twenty years of deep inner half-hearted struggle, he finally decided to give up on his family, and for the second time in his life, to give up on music. He held firm to the first of these resolutions for the rest of his life, and to the second for more than a decade. From the time he left St. Petersburg to the time of his arrival in Vienna in 1777 he

[1] *Memories, Dreams, Reflections*, 1965, p. 346.

moved, when he moved at all, in entirely different circles, spending his time either in virtual seclusion or among illiterates, with the inevitable result that the next chapter is very short.

THE LOST YEARS
(1766–1777)

ALTHOUGH our information on P. D. Q. Bach during the sixteen years preceding 1766 is admittedly extremely meager, it takes on the appearance of a proud Himalayan peak when compared to the diminutive molehill of our information on P. D. Q. Bach during the eleven years following 1766. Having decided to cut the apron strings once and for all, P. D. Q. floated downstream even more aimlessly than before, leaving the Scylla and Charybdis of family and music far behind, and remaining blissfully ignorant of the fact that he would one day return, salmonlike, to the upper reaches of his stream of consciousness, this time to be hopelessly engulfed by the Orphic whirlpool from the periphery of which he had twice before escaped.

Most of what little we do know about this period is based on things that P. D. Q. said or wrote later in his life, things that must obviously be taken with a pillar of salt. Although he felt strongly that melodic lines should not be over-embellished, he had no such scruples concerning the truth, and we would not rely on him so heavily had we other sources from which to choose. It seems highly unlikely, for instance, that he had actually known Catherine the Great before she became great, that is, when she was still the German Princess von Anhalt Zerbst; and yet he always claimed that it was on the basis of "a long-standing acquaintanceship of considerable warmth" that he visited the Empress before leaving St. Petersburg and requested her aid in finding a position. If the "acquaintanceship" was indeed real, it was evidently not as warm as P. D. Q. liked to think, for he spent the next year or so as a boatman on the Volga River.[1] This job came to an end when, after lying down for a short nap on a raft that worked its way loose from its mooring, he overslept and woke up in the middle of the Caspian Sea. Eventually he made his way to Turkey, where he found employment with an Oriental rug-maker, starting out as an assistant warper and working his way up to the position of head woofer.

Several of P. D. Q.'s compositions, though written many years later, bear testimony to the deep impression made upon him by the Near East. The third movement of the *Pervertimento,* marked "Minaret and Trio," the use of the Double Reed Hookah in *The Civilian Barber,* and the as yet undiscovered liturgical work which caused its composer so much trouble with both Protestant and Catholic authorities, the *Mass in the Allah Mode*—these are but a few of the few instances of Oriental orientation within the Occidentally accidental structure of P. D. Q. Bach's music.

Aside from the fact that he nearly drowned trying to dog-paddle across the Hellespont, we know virtually nothing of P. D. Q.'s stay in Turkey. It ended when he breathlessly signed on as a sailor aboard a Bohemian merchant vessel, after making the nearly fatal mistake of penetrating the harem of an unusually vicious and watchful sultan whose amorous deficiencies caused him to be known as the Grand Impotentate.

During the next few years he apparently touched the coast of every country on the Mediterranean Sea, including that of Bohemia itself. But there were two drawbacks to his new life: the work was hard, and he never did find his sea legs. Consequently, he jumped ship in Marseilles and spent some time in the "delightful" nearby town of Bordelleaux. After a few months he tired of the "Rhone maidens," as he called them, and crossed the Pyrenees into Spain, where he made one of the most surprising decisions of his life.

In a rare letter written to an old Dudeldorf friend, P. D. Q. announced his intention to remain in Spain:

The atmosphere in this country is one of relaxation, almost indolence, and this as you know suits my nature perfectly. The peacefulness I have found here extends into my very soul, and indeed I have followed the example of my brother Christian and my cousin Piggy, by converting to the Church of Rome, on the subject of which the Spaniards are very persuasive. Just as I have brought my body to rest after years of

---

[1] He also claimed that he and a fellow worker composed the famous "Song of the Volga Boatman," but since we have ample evidence that P. D. Q. was incapable of carrying a tune and didn't know Russian, the only part he is likely to have composed is the grunt after each phrase, a contribution which does not seem of sufficient significance to warrant the inclusion of the song among P. D. Q.'s *opera,* although he did use the melody as a subject in the "Fuga Vulgaris" from the *Toot Suite.*

wandering and working, so have I decided to bring my soul to rest, and in order to accomplish this worthy goal I feel that I must turn my back upon the worldly world—next week I am entering one of the religious orders, and I intend to spend the rest of my days in a cloister on the Ebro River.

The news that P. D. Q. was taking the holy orders naturally came as a great surprise to his family, since as a child he would never take orders from anyone;[1] it was soon discovered, however, that the "cloister on the Ebro River" was not a monastery, but a nunnery, and P. D. Q. was obliged to make yet another hasty departure, in spite of the pleadings of his cellmates.[2] Although this sacred interlude in his life had a typically profane ending, P. D. Q. did remain a Catholic until his excommunication many years later.

Finally, in the fall of 1777, P. D. Q. found himself in Vienna. Whether his presence there was haphazard, or whether it was motivated by some subconscious desire to surround himself once more with music, we cannot say, but soon after his arrival, in spite of the vow he had observed so faithfully for over ten years, his family's name drew him back into his family's art, this time with results that threatened to ruin both.

---

[1] except when he was a waiter in a Leipzig café, and even then only begrudgingly.

[2] When the full story reached the family, Piggy wrote to Johann Christian: "I knew all along that there was something *fischig* about the reformation of your brother—believe me, if I had been elected Pope this wouldn't have been allowed to happen."

THE TURNING POINT
(1777)

IT seems clear that P. D. Q. Bach had no conscious thought of resuming the pursuit of music when he arrived in Vienna; indeed it is unlikely that he had any conscious thoughts at all, since by his own account he was totally inebriated for the first two weeks of his stay. Having indulged in "that alchemy by which hard cash is transformed into a soft liquid of such potent solvency that even the insolvent may be dissolved," he decided one morning to sober up and think of a way to "transform a minimum amount of effort into a maximum amount of money." That very afternoon the hand of Fate stepped forward.

This was accomplished through the person of Johann Christian Kittel, with whom P. D. Q. had struck up a conversation in a café, being unable to recall where he had seen the naggingly familiar face before; when P. D. Q. mentioned his name, Kittel asked, "Are you by any chance related to the musical Bachs?", and when P. D. Q. identified himself further, Kittel jumped up from his chair exclaiming, "Well, thunderweather! I studied with your father! Why, I remember you—you were the little boy running around without any name!" In the course of their conversation Kittel said that he was organist in the town of Erfurt, but that he was in Vienna doing business with the Baron Gottfried van Swieten, "business which may very well interest yourself, Herr Bach, since it involves your grossly and unjustly neglected father."

Baron van Swieten, who had just become Director of the Imperial Court Library, had spent the previous seven years in Berlin as Imperial *chargé d'affaires* at the Prussian Court. It was from Frederick the Great himself (on whose theme the *Musical Offering* was based) that the Baron had first heard of the greatness of Johann Sebastian Bach, whose music, twenty-seven years after his death, was almost totally unperformed and unknown. The Baron's curiosity turned into enthusiasm when he purchased some of the Master's works, and by the time he settled in Vienna he had, at least of the keyboard music, a considerable collection, which he was anxious to enlarge in spite of his miserliness.[1] This, of course, was the purpose of Kittel's visit to Vienna; he told P. D. Q. that he had "happened to come into the possession of several of your father's works while I was studying with him, God keep his soul, and it seemed to me that they would be so much more safely kept in the Baron's library than in my own home, where they are perforce constantly exposed to the dangers of fire, my children, and the dog." He neglected to mention that the Baron was paying him handsomely for the manuscripts, but that wasn't necessary; P. D. Q.'s mind, although still somewhat damp, had already grasped the implications of the situation with respect to his own financial well-being.

Thus it came about that P. D. Q. decided to offer up for sale his family heirloom, the only material inheritance he had received from his father, the last physical remains of his life in Leipzig: the kazoo, which he had carried with him for over a quarter of a century, often as his only possession. If Van Swieten really worshiped Sebastian Bach as much as Kittel said he did, he would undoubtedly pay a pretty penny for an instrument which in all likelihood had touched the lips of the great Bach himself, and (P. D. Q. must have reasoned) it might even be possible to persuade him that certain other newly acquired artifacts in his possession had actually been part of the household in Leipzig. Kittel offered to take P. D. Q. to the Baron's house the following Sunday; Van Swieten had invited a small group of musicians and connoisseurs to join him in reading through some of the music of Bach and Handel in his collection, a musical afternoon which was later to become a weekly institution. It was incidentally through this institution, some five years later, that Wolfgang Amadeus Mozart, having by then given up any idea of a career in billiards, first discovered the music of J. S. Bach in any quantity, resulting in a creative crisis almost as acute as that which P. D. Q. Bach was about to go through himself.

On the evening of that fateful Sunday, December 2, 1777, Baron van Swieten wrote a letter to King Frederick describing the events of the afternoon. After the usual complimentary modes of address, the Baron starts on the bottom of the third page to report his experience:

The reason this letter follows so closely upon the heels of its predecessor is to be found in a meeting I had earlier today, a meeting so extraordinary that I felt I should record its details immediately, lest I later begin

---

[1] For an interesting but totally incredible explanation of his miserliness see Lars Sorenson, *Early Explorations in the Yukon Territory*, London, 1911.

to doubt my memory. I had organized a small gathering of musicians and educated persons for the purpose of enabling them to acquaint themselves with the musical wonders to which Your Highness so wisely and graciously led me, and which have filled me with so much admiration, even pleasure, during the last several years; I am speaking, of course, of the works of Johann Sebastian Bach. One of the guests was a certain Kittel, who studied with Bach in Leipzig, and from whom I am in the process of purchasing several Bach manuscripts. This Kittell, upon arriving, announced that he had brought someone quite special along with him: the youngest son of Sebastian Bach, younger even than the English Bach, indeed, the last of old Bach's children. An expression of surprise escaped the lips of everyone present; why had none of us heard of this P. D. Q. (I am still ignorant as to what these initials stand for)? Does he too write music? Certainly he must—why then has he remained unknown, when his brothers are among the most honored musicians in all of Europe? We realized that as we were allowing ourselves to speculate in this manner, the one person who could answer our questions was standing out in the hallway waiting to be admitted, and it was with a strong feeling of anticipation that I dispatched a servant to show him in. Just as the servant disappeared, Kittel, who in spite of his interesting news seemed to have an embarrassed air about him, stepped forward and said, "Perhaps I should mention, your Lordship, that in crossing the courtyard Herr Bach had the misfortune to fall into one of the fountains."

I doubt, your Highness, that I shall ever again witness a sight such as that which greeted my eyes when the doors were opened. Standing in a puddle already too large to leap across and still expanding, covered from head to foot with mud (the fountains were not properly cared for by my predecessor), stood a man of average height and, as far as one could tell, unremarkable, perhaps even indiscriminate features. He was rather heavyset, and seemed disinclined to move. His clothes would have required much more than a mere rinsing to render them clean, and the strands of his peruke had come uncurled and hung down on his shoulders, giving him the appearance of a mermaid stranded on the beach. For a long time he just stood there, in one hand holding a small box, in the other a frog, until finally—the rest of us being equally unable, so intense was our astonishment, to speak or move—the Countess von Schrumpfennase fainted dead away, narrowly escaping serious injury, which is more than can be said for Josef Sägen's violin.

The Countess had been standing in front of my fine two-manual harpsichord, which instrument was first made visible to our visitor by her fall to the floor; the moment he laid eyes on it, this Bach, who had been up until then merely immobile, became transfixed. The difference was at first imperceptible, but gradually his eyes opened wide, he dropped the frog, and he began to move toward the harpsichord with slow, soggy steps. Sägen had rushed to where the Countess lay, and was in the process of trying to get the remains of his violin out from under her without doing anything that might be misinterpreted were she suddenly to regain consciousness, when Bach, completely oblivious to everything around him, stepped over her limp body, drenching her so thoroughly that she did indeed awake and immediately slapped poor Sägen, who retreated to the other side of the room clutching a small portion of his violin.

Upon reaching his destination, this son of the most

accomplished musician since Orpheus gazed down at the keyboard, pulled out the bench and seated himself. The eyes of everyone in the room, even the Countess, were fixed upon him, and Your Highness can imagine our surprise when he proceeded to remove his shoes and stockings, and, to my utter horror, started playing with his feet, treating my exquisite harpsichord as if it were a sturdy riding horse that is reluctant to leave the harmonious pasture of music for the tangled forest of cacophony, but is powerless to resist the urging of its insane master.

The counterpoint of aimless tones and dripping water so offended my ears that it jolted me from the trance which had held me motionless, speechless, and incredulous for what seemed like hours; I summoned my senses together and sent for my chief bouncer, Muskelberg, after which I joined Kittel, Sägen, and the others in assisting the Countess to her feet. This turned out to be, like the Countess herself, a job of considerable proportions, and requiring so much effort and concentration that none of us noticed that the music—which term I use in spite of the fact that it makes a perjury of my claim to be giving a truthful account—the music had ceased; when Muskelberg arrived, and the Countess was on the couch, I suddenly became aware of the silence in the room. I turned around, ready to put Muskelberg to work, only to discover that his task had already been accomplished by our visitor himself; the harpsichord was down on the floor, its legs having collapsed, the bench was empty, and there was a trail of water leading to the open windows. Herr Bach had evidently forgotten that he was on the third floor—all the ivy between the windows and the ground had been torn from the walls and was piled up in the garden below, almost but not quite obscuring a small crater in the dirt; Bach

himself, however, was nowhere to be seen, and I suspect, nay pray, that I have seen the last of him.

I fear that I have taken up too much of Your Highness' valuable time, but I thought that you would be as interested as I in seeing that a sow's ear could be produced from a silk purse, as it were; you may rest assured, however, that my researches into the music of the Olympian Bach will continue unabated, for the insignificance of the molehill only serves to enhance the loftiness of the mountain.

Written in haste, but with all due respects, and apologies for anything that may be troubling Your Highness, I remain

yr hmbl & obdnt svnt
Baron Gottfried van Swieten

I have reproduced this letter virtually in its entirety because, in addition to giving a very clear idea of exactly what it was about P. D. Q. Bach that made such a strong impression on people, it also marks one of the most important turning points in his life. One cannot fail to notice what an effect seeing a harpsichord had on P. D. Q. after eleven years of artless wandering, just as one cannot fail to be impressed by the intense concentration of which he was capable in spite of his lack of discipline; according to the Baron, he was "completely oblivious to everything around him" from the moment he saw the instrument until, one assumes, the moment it collapsed, at which point his mind must have returned to practical, everyday concerns within a matter of seconds.

In a letter to his Dudeldorf friend, P. D. Q. describes the visit to Van Swieten's as a "revelation," because "I suddenly realized that while I was struggling on the banks of the Volga, and warping and woofing sixteen hours a day in the Turkish heat, and staggering around on the deck of that wretched ship, in short, while I was ruining my health and denying my natural temperament by working, my brothers were sitting around taking it easy, dashing off a piece now and then, nothing difficult—I have for years rebelled against everything for which my family stands, but since it has occurred to me that they have practically monopolized one of the softest ways to make a living there is, rebelling no longer seems worth the effort."

As a result of these reflections, P. D. Q. Bach started writing music, probably for the first time in his life. He was thirty-five years old, the age at which Mozart died,[1] and he had not concerned himself with any aspect of music, as far as we know, since the age of twenty-two. He had a good ear, but his other one was really terrible, and any account of his life that fails to mention the fact that one of his ears was slightly pointed would have to be considered seriously deficient. He had never had any formal musical training, and the few musicians with whom he came into contact after his eighth year were either mavericks or openly hostile. All these things show in his music. But the larger question remains unanswered: Was the mind that formed the musical style itself formed by the formative years herein described, or was the nature of those formative years formed by the mind that formed the musical style? The author doesn't know much about psychology, but he knows what he likes, and his own answer to that question is unequivocal: It all depends on how you look at it. First, you have

[1] See Baker's Biographical Dictionary of Musicians, 4th Edition, New York, 1940.

to define your terms. For instance, what do you mean by "form"? Do you mean "form" in the sense of "formulate" or in the sense of "shape"? The latter implies an unconscious causality whereas the former (and what does "former" mean? One who forms?) implies a conscious mental exercise, something that temporal units such as years obviously could not be said to be capable of performing (here again we are faced with a wide variety of meanings, due this time not only to the vagueness of "form" but also to various effects upon "form" of the diverse meanings of the prefix "per": throughout in space or time, away, over, completely, thoroughly, extremely, very, etc.). Furthermore, the whole question of heredity vs. environment has not been treated thoroughly as it applies to composers' styles, as opposed to the considerable attention it has received at the hands of scientists interested merely in the basic problems of human behavior. Is there, for instance, any connection between Brahms' orchestration and his mother's hatred of washing windows? Is the fact that both of Johann Sebastian Bach's parents died when he was a boy of ten the reason that the composer never wrote ten of anything, but always six or twelve or forty-eight? And has any scholar explored the possibility that Beethoven, having had a grandfather who was a bass and a father who was a tenor, grew up with a subconscious urge to sing alto so overpowering that his vocal cords were under a constant strain, leading eventually to headaches, colic, death, and possibly even syphilis? And what, actually, is the nature of causality? In logical argument the phrase "it follows that . . ." is often heard, and yet of course it does not necessarily follow that the fact that one thing follows another is proof of causation on the part of the one thing with respect to the other. Certainly the fact that Jacques Offenbach was followed, temporally, by Franz Kafka does not mean that Offenbach *caused* Kafka in any biological sense of the term; one could, however, argue that the cultural *environment* in part created (i.e., caused) by Offenbach's *actions* (which were deter-

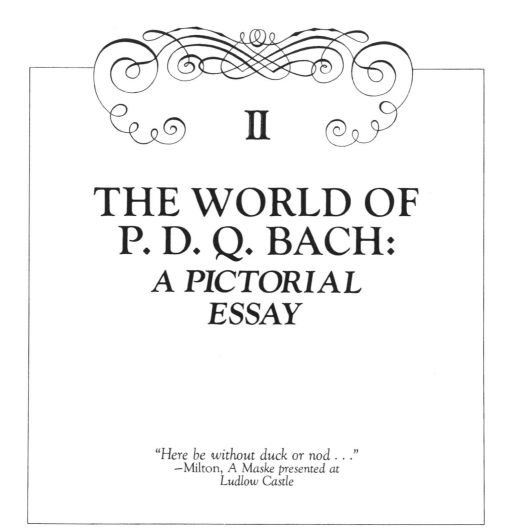

II

THE WORLD OF P. D. Q. BACH:
A PICTORIAL ESSAY

"Here be without duck or nod . . ."
—Milton, A Maske presented at
Ludlow Castle

P. D. Q. Bach was as unusual among eighteenth-century composers as eighteenth-century composers were among him. And yet in the broadest sense he was produced by the same world that produced Haydn and Mozart and all the lesser but nevertheless competent composers that dotted the musical landscape of the Age of Enlightenment; P. D. Q. simply chose (or was forced, depending on one's interpretation of the facts presented in Part I) to inhabit different areas of that world, areas that Haydn and Mozart and all the lesser but nevertheless competent composers that dotted the musical landscape of the Age of Enlightenment would never have gone near, at least not after nightfall.

The present author had considered titling Part II "The World of P. D. Q. Bach As He Saw It," but further reflection yielded the realization that reproducing a set of pictures in a manner that would be faithful to such a title would present almost insurmountable technical difficulties, since for the greater part of his life P. D. Q. rarely saw less than two of anything he looked at. The better part of valor, therefore, seemed to dictate a more modest approach; wherever possible we will, however, be looking at P. D. Q. and his surroundings, both animate and inanimate, through the eyes of his contemporaries.

PLATE 1

This portrait, the only true portrait of P. D. Q. Bach in existence, was done in the late 1770's by Franz Romanssohn Kontrimänn. It escaped almost certain destruction by the rest of the Bach family only because the penurious artist, having grown impatient waiting for P. D. Q. to pay for his picture, simply painted over it for a new, more trustworthy client. The original subject of the canvas might never have been discovered had not the painting been stolen from the Tate Gallery in 1964, for upon its recovery it was x-rayed as part of the authentication procedure, and the facing face emerged. The present author, having read in a newspaper account that the canvas bore the "enigmatic" intials "P. D. Q." in the lower left-hand corner, rushed to London and was able to establish beyond a doubt the identity of the man whose image had lain submerged under that of a minor German official for almost two centuries. The Tate Gallery refused to strip off the outer portrait, but in 1968 the painting was again stolen from the Gallery, and this remarkable likeness of P. D. Q. Bach now hangs in the P. D. Q. Bach Museum at the University of Southern North Dakota at Hoople.

PLATE 2

Leipzig, the birthplace of P. D. Q. Bach, as it looked two hundred years ago.

PLATE 3

Leipzig as it looks today. Gone is the feeling of spaciousness that characterized the city during the eighteenth century.

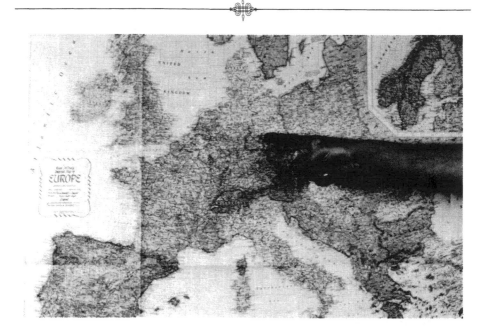

PLATE 4

St. Thomas' Church in Leipzig. P. D. Q. Bach's father was Cantor and *Director Musices* at the church for the last twenty-seven years of his life. He lived and taught in the school building at the left, and it was here that P. D. Q. was born. The story, first reported by Forkel, that the infant was thrown into the fountain at the right by his parents, who, when they noticed that they had been observed, fished him out again, claiming that they were merely "practicing up" for the boy's baptism, is almost certainly apochryphal. Although he may have been passionately ignored, there is no evidence to suggest that P. D. Q. Bach suffered physical cruelty at the hands of his parents. Their feet is a different matter.

PLATE 5

Johann Sebastian Bach, P. D. Q.'s father, considered by many to be the greatest composer who ever lived. This is one of the most famous portraits of J. S. Bach.

(33)

PLATE 6

Another portrait of J. S. Bach, done shortly after the birth of P. D. Q.

PLATE 7

P. D. Q.'s mother was Anna Magdalena Bach, J. S. Bach's second wife. Hardly less prolific than her Olympian husband, she bore him fifteen children and played the harpsichord fairly well, considering how little time she had to practice. The author was unable to find a portrait of Anna Magdalena, but if Johann Sebastian was lucky, she might have looked something like the French singer Marie Armand, pictured here.

PLATE 8

Wilhelm Friedemann Bach, P. D. Q.'s half-brother and the eldest son of Johann Sebastian. He inherited a generous helping of his father's talent, but shared P. D. Q.'s predilection for the bottle. Perhaps due to this common bond, he was the only member of the Bach family who showed any sympathy whatsoever toward P. D. Q.; indeed the infamous masked *Säuferpaar* (Drunken Duo) that so offended the tastes of the citizens of Halle during the summer of 1765 may very well have been none other than the youngest and eldest sons of the most devoutly religious composer of the eighteenth century. The Bach family always maintained that Wilhelm Friedemann gave up his position as Music Director and Organist at Halle voluntarily, but recent scholars have argued persuasively that he was in fact removed from his post, probably in a wheelbarrow.

When Wilhelm Friedemann died in 1784 at the age of seventy-four, P. D. Q. traveled to Berlin for the funeral, and wore the label from a bottle of W. F.'s favorite wine as an armband for six weeks.

PLATES 9 AND 10

This group portrait of the Bach family at home is perhaps over-roman-
ticized, but it is extremely valuable to us because it is the earliest picture
we have of P. D. Q. Bach (see detail). Unfortunately, he has crawled
under the covers, displaying, even at the tender age of one, the antipathy
toward music that was to shape his style as a composer many years later.
The various members of the family are identified in the diagram below.

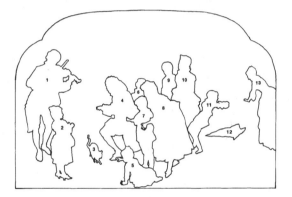

1. Gottfried Heinrich
2. Johanna Carolina
3. Tabbias Thomas Felix
4. Johann Sebastian
5. Regine Susanna
6. Johann August Abraham[1]
7. Johann Christian

8. Elisabeth Juliana Friderica
9. Johann Christoph Friedrich
10. Same as No. 8
11. Bubele Bach, a nephew
12. P. D. Q.
13. None of the above

[1] Most biographers state that J.A.A. Bach died in infancy, but actually he was simply
lost in the shuffle.

PLATE 11

Little P. D. Q. at the feet of a paternal great-granduncle on his father's side, Lips Bach. Already well over one hundred and fifty years old by the time P. D. Q. was born, Lips had been a carpet-maker by trade, but his passion was the trumpet, and he kept in such remarkable shape that he was able to play taps at his own funeral in 1905. His astonishingly rugged body housed a friendly, easygoing spirit, a quality also found in his faithful companion, Woofgang. It was from the latter, by the way, that P. D. Q. received his first (and, in all likelihood, only) musical training.

PLATES 12 AND 13

That P. D. Q. himself showed considerable talent for drawing is demonstrated by his fanciful additions to an early portrait of his father. Since it is well known that Johann Sebastian had trouble with his eyesight, the painting as it appears at the left was accepted as a true, if slightly surprising, likeness of the Master, until the development of modern spectographic analysis proved that the glasses, mustache and beard are later embellishments, done (according to the amazingly precise calculations now possible through carbon-dating), on the 29th of July, 1750, the day after J. S. Bach died. The entry in the diary of P. D. Q.'s sister Johanna Carolina for that day, "*Item:* What well-known twerp's pen has no respect for the dead?" leaves little room for speculation as to the identity of the culprit.

PLATE 14

The only instrument upon which P. D. Q. Bach was an acknowledged virtuoso was the wine bottle. It was the only instrument he practiced every day, and this drawing indicates that he started practicing at an early age. Many years later he was to compose what are commonly regarded as the most idiomatic wine bottle solos ever written, in his infamous cantata *Iphigenia in Brooklyn* (see page 196). The cantata, incidentally, employs an alto instrument, not the *bottiglia bassa* shown opposite.

PLATE 15

When P. D. Q. was eight years old, his father died. This picture of
Johann Sebastian going up to heaven was done by an eyewitness to the
event, who said that the sky was filled with "the most glorious music, as
if God himself were playing upon the great Organ of the Cosmos, and
really playing up a storm, too." The following month a eulogy appeared
in the official publication of the Guild of Church Musicians, *The Organ
Organ*, expressing the "deeply felt" sentiments of "each and every" member of the guild: "That Sebastian Bach was the King of Instruments there
can be no denying and we must all experience the pang of his passing.
We must not, however, cease to strive for the lofty ideals that continued
to inspire him as long as he was (as the expression is among organists)
alive and kicking; life must, and no doubt will, go on. Although the
world has lost a great musician, it has gained a vacancy; applications are
now being accepted by the Leipzig Town Council."

PLATE 16

The only picture we have of Ludwig Zahnstocher, the extraordinary musician/inventor to whom P. D. Q. was apprenticed in 1755, and whose letters are quoted extensively in Part I, is this print showing the two of them at work on the Pandemonium, which Zahnstocher called (justly, it would seem) "the loudest instrument ever created upon the earth." The older man is standing on top of the beam, while P. D. Q., perhaps (judging by the expression on his face) just becoming aware of what is going to happen when the cut is completed, saws from underneath. Zahnstocher was so proud of the Pandemonium that he had an English translation of the plans for the instrument made, which he sent off to his friend Dr. Charles Burney in London (see page 89), hoping that the soon-to-be-famous musical historian might be able to arrange a tour of the British Isles for the instrument and its inventors. The idea, like the instrument itself, came to naught.

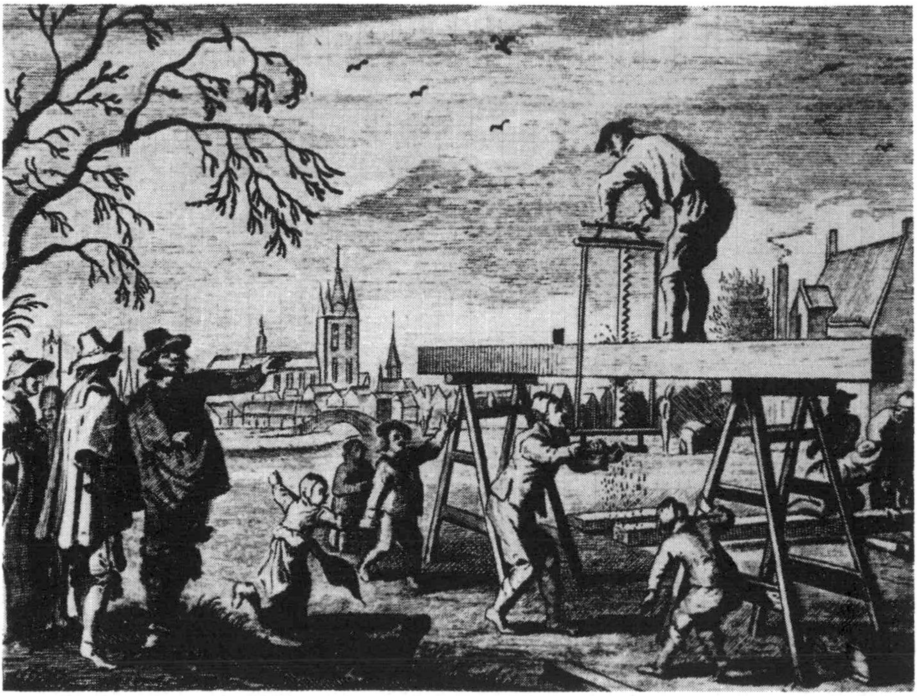

PLATE 17

Zahnstocher's diagram of the Pandemonium is more or less self-explanatory, but a few clarifying comments are in order: The organ pipe (a) was constructed so that the air escaped from the top (rather than from the side, as is usually the case) of the pipe, thus making possible the catapult effect indicated. The sound of the organ pipe was described as "ear-shattering and very loud" by P. D. Q., and may actually have caused some of the aural dysfunctions that one is forced to consider when one is trying to explain certain aspects of P. D. Q. Bach's music. The two chutes contained spring-mounted slats made of (l) wood and (f) metal that snapped noisily back into position as the cannonballs passed through them. Also, in trying to imagine the sound of the Pandemonium, it must be borne in mind that the diagram is only a cross-section; the full instrument had twenty-five of each part shown in the drawing.

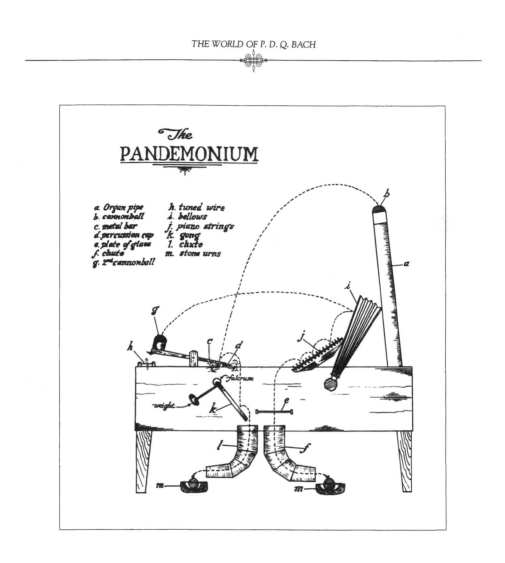

PLATE 18

P. D. Q.'s sojourn to Dublin and London began, as far as we can tell, when the boy was about twenty years old. We have seen that, even at a much younger age, he was no stranger to the bottle, but this inn bill shows that his drinking habits had assumed gargantuan proportions by the time he attained his majority. The bill was found among some personal effects left behind by P. D. Q. when he climbed out the back window of the inn to avoid paying it.

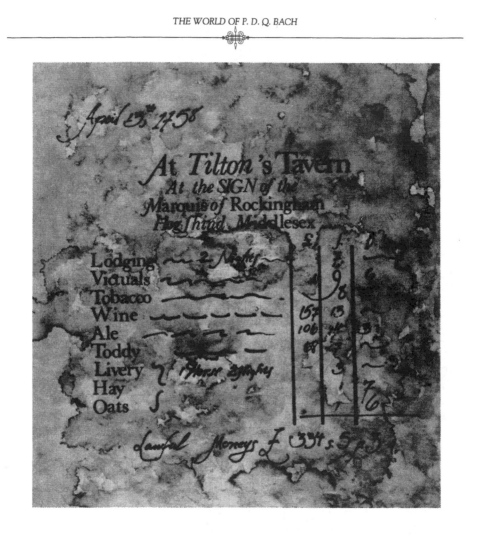

PLATE 19

Johann Christian Bach was Johann Sebastian's next-to-youngest son, having been born several years before P. D. Q. Although rarely played today, he was one of the most popular composers of his time, succeeding Handel as music-master to the Queen of England before his thirtieth birthday, and his music had a profound influence upon that of Mozart, which is more than you can say for Brahms. At the height of his success in London, J. C. had an extraordinary house built for himself in the shape of a grand church organ; in the drawing opposite we see him looking out of his window at two of the many *Gruppien* who hung around outside at all hours, hoping to be invited in by the young master. When P. D. Q. showed up in London in 1763 or 4, he obviously had high hopes that J. C. would fix him up, if not with a job, at least with a double date.

(57)

PLATE 20

Whether Johann Christian made his younger brother sign this agreement because he had heard about the staggering bills (such as the one on page 55) that P. D. Q. was wont to run up, or simply because he wanted to encourage P. D. Q. to leave soon, we can only surmise. P. D. Q. probably enlisted the aid of his sister-in-law, whom he called "Sis" Boom Bach and with whom he was extremely friendly, in working out the wording of the agreement (which J. C. must not have bothered to read very carefully), since his own knowledge of the English language at this point was limited to conversational phrases such as "water closet" and "elephant."

I hereby acknowledge that I owe J. Christian Bach thruppence, that is to say 8 pence, in return for which he agrees to provide the undersigned for three days with bed and broad.

P.D.Q. Bach

London, [illegible]

PLATE 21

When P. D. Q. heard about a job opening and asked his brother Johann Christian for a testimonial, or (as we would now call it) letter of recommendation, J. C. took advantage of the fact that P. D. Q. read very little English and produced the document reproduced here.

Whereas the bearer, Mr. P. D. Q. Bach has requested me, the undersign'd, to give him an Impartial Testimony concerning his learning in the Art of Musick, and also his abilities in performing the Fruits of said Art, so that he may be granted permission to apply in person for the recently vacated post of Temporary Substitute Assistant Organist at St. Jezebel's Cathedral in Haymarket; now therefore I have not wish'd to deny him the same, but must, in all good Conscience, do that very thing, for, though the bearer makes claim to be a relative of mine on our Father's and Mother's side, yet never have I met a person whom the Muses have so mercifully ignor'd, a person, advertising himself a musician, so completely devoid of the ability to affect the emotions by rend'ring Harmony upon the King of Instruments, unless it be the emotion of Disgust, or perhaps, in the feminine breast, that of Pity, in short, a person so unworthy of the name Bach that his very existence must be consider'd an Affront to Taste. I am convinc'd that allowing this person to exhibit his Skills, if such indeed they may be call'd, would be for the worthy recipient of this epistle not merely a Waste of Time, but in sooth an almost criminal Misuse of Time, so little of which is allotted to us here on this mortal Orb.

Joh. Christian Bach
Musick Master to the Queen

London

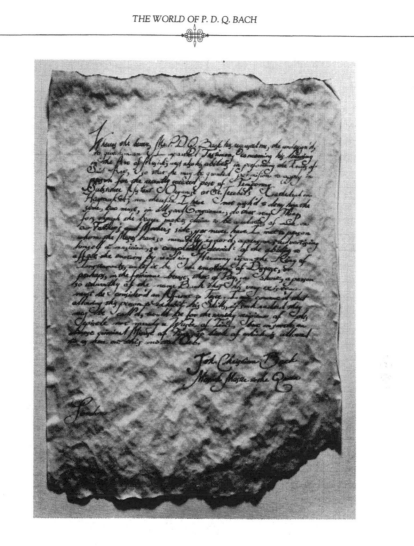

PLATE 22

St. Jezebel's Cathedral today, looking much the same as it did two hundred years ago. To Johann Christian's great surprise, P. D. Q. was actually named to the post of Temporary Substitute Assistant Organist of the Chapel, on the condition that he also cut the grass, take out the garbage, and check the chlorine level in the font. Although he was pleased to have landed the job, P. D. Q. did admit to being disappointed when he found out that the church was located not in Haymarket, London, but in the notorious Haymarket Bog several miles to the north of London; since J. C. had just upped his rent, however, he decided to make the move.

PLATE 23

Within two years, thanks to his having learned some interesting information concerning the Bishop and two chambermaids, P. D. Q. was elected Organist of the Chapel at St. Jezebel's, and the document that he drew up when he accepted the position shows that, in addition to being a musical innovator, P. D. Q. Bach was the first to use small print in a contract.

In return for a Monthly Stipend of five Shillings, which sum is to be paid in full every Monday, I, the undersigned, do agree to play the Organ for all Services and Choir Rehearsals, and in general to perform the Duties incumbent upon the Organist of the Chapel if I feel like it.

P. D. Q. Bach

PLATES 24 AND 25

Betty-Sue Bach, the daughter of P. D. Q.'s St. Petersburg cousin Leonhard Sigismund Dietrich Bach, as she looked (l.) at the time of P. D. Q.'s visit, and (r.) eight and a half months later. Due to an understandable reluctance on the part of the "Russian" Bachs to discuss the subject, nothing is known about the offspring of the two cousins except that the line has continued down to the present day (see Part III), which cannot be said of the legitimate male side of the family.

In 1807, still unmarried, Betty-Sue visited P. D. Q. on his death-floor, at which time he presented her with the *Notebook for Betty-Sue Bach* (see page 202). Betty-Sue never returned to St. Petersburg; after P. D. Q.'s death, she married his friend Jonathan "Boozey" Hawkes, accompanying him when he returned to his native Liverpool to set up a music publishing house. She devoted the last years of her life to overseeing the publication of several of P. D. Q. Bach's works, for which efforts, in 1817, she was burned at the stake.

PLATE 26

Vienna in the eighteenth century. P. D. Q. Bach settled here in 1777, and soon thereafter made the momentous decision that was to change him from an obscure drunk into an obscure drunk composer. Here Fate—or was it perhaps some intangible quality in Vienna's air?[1]—guided P. D. Q. back to Music; by the time he left for smaller ponds he had written the works of his first creative period, the Initial Plunge.

[1] No, it was Fate.

PLATE 27

Baron von Tutti, as his name implies, was of Italian and German ancestry. Known to his friends as "Cozy," he was among those present at
the Baron van Swieten's on the day of P. D. Q. Bach's memorable visit
(see page 16), and, anxious to start his own collection of Bachanalia, he
had lost no time in seeking P. D. Q. out immediately afterward, probably
by following the trail of water leading from the crater in the garden
under the third-story window to the nearest tavern. Apparently he could
hold his own as a beer-drinker with any commoner, and he did not affect
the haughty aristocratic airs of Van Swieten, so when he met P. D. Q. at
the Sign of the Boar's Head, they hit it off immediately; the owner made
them hang it up again, but allowed them to stay, and the two men sat
and drank until well after midnight, slowly becoming fast friends.

(71)

PLATE 28

It was through the Baron "Cozy" von Tutti that P. D. Q. made the acquaintance of Thomas Pollex, a diminutive young man whose voice so resembled that of a baby bird that it earned him the nickname "Peeping Tom,"[1] much to the consternation of his father. Castor N. Pollex ran a toy shop, but he was passionately devoted to music, and his son's music lessons (see illustration) began shortly after the boy was born. Ear training took precedence over toilet training, and the infant Tom first learned to stand up by holding on to a flute that his father had suspended from the ceiling like a trapeze. It has even been suggested that Tom's small stature as an adult was due to the fact that as a child he was forced to affect a flute embouchure (mouth position) at all times, making it difficult to get any but the smallest bits of food into his mouth. It is small wonder, then, that growing up (to the extent that he did) in his father's shop, Peeping Tom became a virtuoso not only on the flute *(flauto dolce)*, but also on the ocarina *(patata dolce)*, the slide whistle, the nose flute, the Oscar Mayer wiener whistle, and many other musical toys too whimsical to mention. Small wonder, too, that he was delighted with the idea of having a concerto composed specifically to show off his dexterity with a great variety of instruments. And small wonder that, after performing P. D. Q.'s *Gross Concerto*, he became known as the Small Wonder.

[1] An aphorism coined by Professor David Robinson of Ohio State University, "Samuel Pepys where angels fear to whisper," is of little relevance here.

PLATE 29

The story of Peeping Tom Pollex ends on a sad note, or rather it sadly ends on no note. Immediately after the death of his father in 1780 the by-now-famous flautist suddenly announced that he would never touch the flute again, and that he would henceforth open his mouth as far as he wanted to, whenever he wanted to. Imagine his disappointment when he discovered that he had lockjaw; indeed, that he had probably had it for years. With the aid of a chisel he finally managed to pry his mouth open, and one of the first things he did after looking in the mirror was to engage the services of a portrait painter. The almost delirious nature of his joy is evident in the resulting picture: his eyes shine with an intense—one is tempted to say maniacal—gleam, and he has just bitten off the end of his flute and swallowed it. Unfortunately, two days later his mouth snapped back to its accustomed position, this time never to move again, in spite of the efforts of two doctors, the entire Carpenters' Guild, and a military expert on explosives. Crippled in body and spirit, Pollex spent the rest of his short life developing the modern drinking straw.

PLATE 30

Prince Fred, of the House of Hangover, was a bastard son of George II of England by Lady "Lady" Lady, a well-known bluestocking and bluenose whose husband, Sir Yodah, was a member of Parliament and away on business a lot. The prince was a great lover of music, often singing to the accompaniment of his wife, Princess Polly, who played the harp not only backward, but also upside down and crosswise. On a trip to Vienna in 1777 Prince Fred had heard Thomas Pollex playing on a now-obsolete instrument, the dill piccolo, and he was so enthusiastic about the tiny tooter's virtuosity that when he heard that Pollex was having a concerto composed especially for himself, he (Prince Fred) invited the midget musician to Wein-am-Rhein, offering the use of his orchestra for the premiere performance, in spite of the fact that before talking to the Baron von Tutti he (still Prince Fred) had never heard of the composer. P. D. Q. Bach finished the *Gross Concerto* on the 31st of December, and on New Year's Day, 1778, in the company of Peeping Tom and Cozy, he (P. D. Q. Bach this time) staggered aboard a Western-bound coach, totally oblivious to everything around him as well as to the enormous significance of the week-long trip he was about to sleep through.

PLATE 31

One visit to the town of Wein-am-Rhein, noted principally for producing one of the most robust wines in all of Europe, the famous *Leapfrogmilch,* convinced P. D. Q. that he had at last found a place that suited his temperament. He moved here in January of 1778 and remained for his entire Soused Period, that is, until May of 1807, bound by an affinity he had never felt for any other place. By the end of the eighteenth century, to a remarkable extent, Wein-am-Rhein *was* P. D. Q. Bach, both in the minds of its townspeople and in the minds of the few people in the rest of Europe who had heard of either; and when P. D. Q. died, something in the heart of Wein-am-Rhein died as well; by the middle of the nineteenth century it was virtually a ghost town, inhabited by a few old-timers who would talk for hours, given the slightest encouragement, about the "good old days" *("gute alte Tage")* when the streets were paved with P. D. Q. Bach and his friends—when (as in the eighteenth-century drawing on the opposite page) the river was plied by beer barrels and idle fishermen, and the sky was punctuated by the lofty spires of the world's largest taverns.

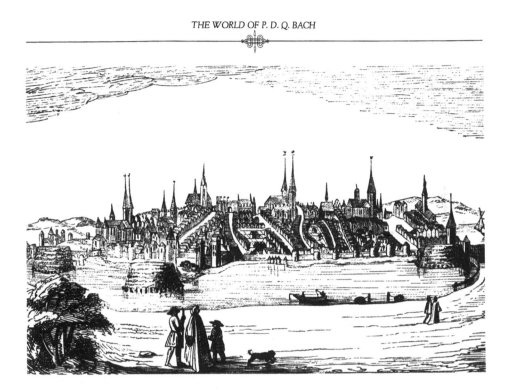

PLATES 32 AND 33

It didn't take P. D. Q. Bach long after his arrival in Wein-am-Rhein to gather around him a circle of friends who were, as was he, selflessly dedicated to the art of drinking and hopelessly addicted to music. Next to P. D. Q. himself, perhaps the most notorious drinker of them all was Thomas Collins, a degenerate debaucher who also happened to be the greatest classical bagpiper of his day. It was for him that P. D. Q. wrote the *Pervertimento,* and this picture of him is exceptionally interesting because in the background (see detail) we can see P. D. Q. himself, either following the score or unwrapping a sandwich.

PLATE 34

In the spring of 1778 a gypsy musician wandered into Wein-am-Rhein with nothing but an old fiddle to his unpronounceable name. His constant use of the object that stands in front of him in this painting earned him a new name, and he also earned something with which to fill his pockets by abducting the entire orchestra of a nearby home for wayward girls; with them he made highly successful tours all over Europe, billed as "Phil Spitoony and his All-Girl Chamber Ensemble," until the 1789 crackdown on white-slave traffic in the German Empire forced his retirement. He spent most of the rest of his life in Wein-am-Rhein trying to dissolve his *Wanderlust* in alcohol and performing in musical *soirées* such as the one pictured here. The way he plays with one foot propped up is a quaint reminder of his beginnings as a guitarist with Mordo Jones and his Gypsy Gentlemen; in fact, when Spitoony died it was discovered that his instrument was not a violin at all, but a modified tenor ukelele built by Arturo Gadfri of Cremona in 1693.

PLATE 35

Porcelina Speck was perhaps the most accomplished keyboard player in Wein-am-Rhein. Born Porcelina Bacon, of an aristocratic English family, she was abandoned by her parents in 1768 during a tour of the Continent, and after wandering around town for a while the sixteen-year-old lass decided to forget about returning to England. She had noticed that, within an hour or two after the opening time of the taverns, a large percentage of the population of Wein-am-Rhein had lost the ability to see clearly, and she undoubtedly reasoned that her odd physical appearance would be less of a handicap here than it had been at home, where, except for an extremely unsavory encounter with a large hog on her uncle's estate, she had had no social life at all.

She and P. D. Q. obviously had at least two things in common: music and their extraordinarily unequivocal rejection by their respective families, and after taking into consideration all the available evidence, one is forced to entertain the possibility that their friendship was not always platonic.[1]

---

[1] It is difficult, for instance, to dismiss the suspicion that the following news item from the Wein-am-Rhein *Schnapsblatt* (Daily Dram) refers to P. D. Q. and Porcelina:

It is rumored that the destruction of the grape arbor in Herr Schwips' backyard is due to a falling out between a well-known local composer and an equally well-known local clavecinist. Actually the falling out was performed by the composer, who (it is said) leaned too far out of his paramour's window while relieving himself, with the result that he also relieved his paramour of his presence.

PLATE 36

Not all of P. D. Q.'s friends were musicians; many were professionals in other fields.

PLATE 37

Dr. Charles Burney was one of the leading musical historians of the eighteenth century. His *General History of Music* was published in four volumes between 1776 and 1789, and although his extensive trips throughout Europe in 1770 and 1772 formed the principal basis for his personal observations, he did make a brief journey in 1788 in preparation for the final volume of his monumental work.

This trip included a visit to Wein-am-Rhein; he had heard about P. D. Q. Bach from Ludwig Zahnstocher (see page 50) and was anxious to meet this "unknown twig on the Bach family tree." His account of his quest is quoted extensively in Appendix C; suffice it to state here that he started his search, one might say rather naïvely, at the monastery just outside of town, and that the first monk to whom he talked reacted to the mention of P. D. Q. Bach's name by rolling his eyes toward heaven and crossing himself thrice, adding that "in the long history of the Church, P. D. Q. Bach is the only *person* ever to be declared a cardinal sin."

THE METROPOLITAN MUSEUM OF ART, THE CROSBY BROWN COLLECTION, 1901.

PLATE 38

As luck would have it, Padre Martini, the famous composer-cleric, happened to be staying at the monastery. Renowned throughout Europe as a teacher (Mozart and Gluck were among his students), Padre Martini was in Wein-am-Rhein trying, for the sake of the Bach family name, to instill a modicum of musical learning into the humid brain of Johann Sebastian's youngest son. Having decided that he had set himself a hopeless task, he was just packing his bags to return to Bologna, but he gave Burney an address at which, he assured the Englishman, P. D. Q. Bach could be found, "if you look in the corners and under the tables."

PLATE 39

One of the few things that could get P. D. Q. up off the floor was the prospect of an evening of playing and singing through some of the pieces that Prince Fred periodically brought over from his private library, which consisted primarily of works he had commissioned from P. D. Q. and several other even more obscure composers.

These musical *soirées* usually began late in the afternoon at Dufay's Tavern and ended around daybreak at the police station. The document at the right, a page from the Wein-am-Rhein police blotter, shows that on the 6th of December 1791 several of P. D. Q.'s friends were fined 8 *Groschen* for drunkenness, while P. D. Q. himself was fined 10 *Thaler* 12 *Groschen* for "unbelievable drunkenness."

Polizeiwache Wein-am-Rhein

	Geldstrafen		6 Dezember 1791
Holz, Gustav		8 gr	Trunkenheit
Colums, Thomas		8 gr	Trunkenheit
Zoll, Anton		8 gr	Trunkenheit
Hawkes, "Boosey"		8 gr	Trunkenheit
Adler, Molly		8 gr	Trunkenheit
Bach, P.D.Q.		10 rth 12 gr	Unglaubliche Trunkenheit

PLATES 40 AND 41

Of course it took a good deal of money to maintain this *modus vivendi*. Although Prince Fred did commission P. D. Q. every now and then to write a work to celebrate some family occasion such as one of his sons losing a tooth, or even some municipal occasion such as the opening of the Brewery of the Madonna, these commissions were certainly insufficient to support P. D. Q.; gradually he began to realize that he would have to find some extramusical way of supplementing his income. Surprisingly enough, the method he chose turned out to be highly successful; in the spring of 1795 the P. D. Q. Bach Traveling Medicine Show left Wein-am-Rhein, and by the time it returned eight months later, P. D. Q. was a wealthy man.

One of the main ingredients of his success was undoubtedly the fact that he employed a singer (seen in the top picture wearing a pointed hat and in the bottom picture dancing), for whom he composed a series of *Diverse Ayres*, as he called them, which were actually singing commercials—perhaps the first singing commercials in history (see page 199).

PLATE 42

It was presumably on one of his business trips that P. D. Q. Bach met Beethoven in Vienna. The introduction was arranged through one of the great composer's cousins, Moe Beethoven, whom P. D. Q. had met in Bonn many years earlier. Ludwig had always been particularly fond of this cousin—he used to refer to him affectionately as his "Bonn Moe"—and he was glad to oblige him by meeting an old friend. It was the last time Ludwig ever did a favor for Moe, for once P. D. Q. had met the master, every time he was in town he would show up at Beethoven's apartment, after having stood in the street for a while making careful note of the noble strains wafting from the window; as soon as he entered the room he would take a swig out of Beethoven's fifth, sit down at the piano, and proceed to inflict his latest piece upon his captive audience. Among the things P. D. Q. picked up from Beethoven were a fondness for violent contrast, several pieces of silverware, and the practice (shown opposite) of writing music on his sleeve when no paper was handy.

PLATE 43

Prince Fred's country castle, the infamous Schlampampenschloss (Make Merry Manor), situated about a mile southeast of Wein-am-Rhein. At the end of the Prince's bacchanalian all-night revels, any departing guests who were unable to negotiate stairs were shown to the shaft in the center. As they stepped into the empty tower their host pressed a button marked DOWN, which caused the bottom of the shaft to be filled with 500 pounds of goose feathers, thus averting an unpleasant end to an otherwise enjoyable evening.

In this castle began the climactic event of P. D. Q. Bach's life in Wein-am-Rhein. On the 30th of April 1807, about a month after P. D. Q. turned sixty-five, Prince Fred honored him with a concert, billed as a "P. D. Q. Bach Retrogressive," in the Great Hall of the Schlampampenschloss. All of P. D. Q.'s friends, even the most disreputable, were invited, and they all managed to get themselves up the hill to the castle. No fewer than ten works were listed on the program, but an altercation broke out during the *Echo Sonata for Two Unfriendly Groups of Instruments,* which opened the concert, and before long the entire assemblage had joined in a riotous free-for-all that threatened to destroy the castle completely. Fearing just such an end to the evening, Prince Fred suggested that the concert be resumed at the establishment of Madame Höllender, which suggestion was greeted with unanimous agreement.

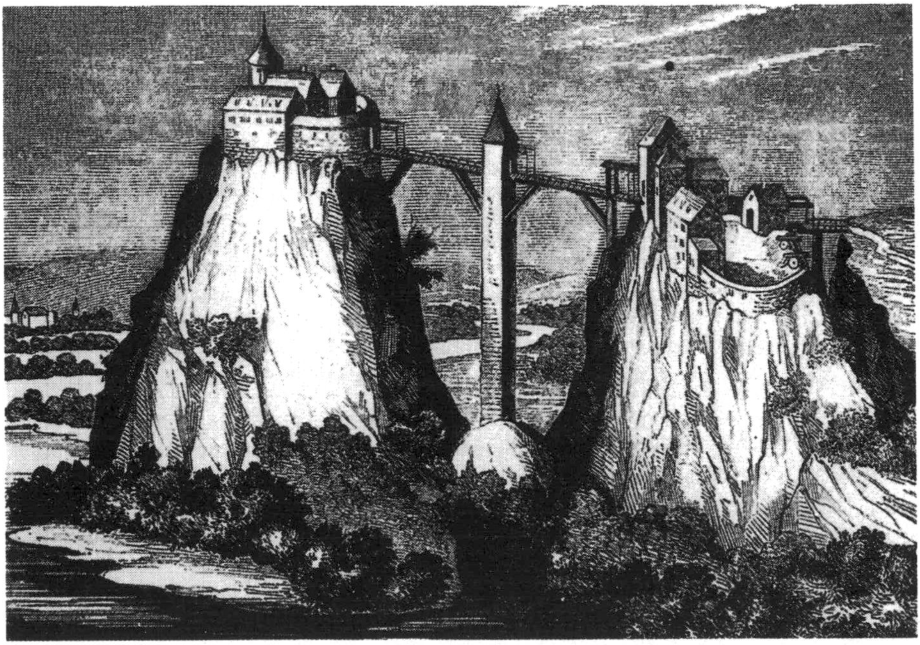

PLATE 44

By the time the motley group of musicians, singers, and listeners arrived at Madame Höllender's, the violence that had so marred the concert at Prince Fred's palace had been forgotten; in fact, so had the concert. In the accompanying engraving P. D. Q. Bach can be seen just to the right of center, eating and drinking with the proprietress; on the left, with the two "waitresses," is Enrico Carouso, the notorious bargain counter tenor for whom P. D. Q. wrote most of his vocal works, and whose inability to sire offspring made him especially popular with women. The man on the right is the mayor of Wein-am-Rhein, who evidently turned his back when he saw that a sketch was being made, and just beyond him are the miter and staff of Bishop Walburga. He too has seen the artist at work, and has retired behind the folding screen on the left, upon which hangs his chasuble. According to the reminiscences of one of the participants,[1] Bishop Walburga reemerged as soon as the picture was completed; he not only joined in the festivities but even, when Madame Höllender ran out of wine, invited the entire company over to his Church, where, he claimed, were to be had the "very best wines in Christendom."

[1] *Pipes and Ale: The Memoirs of Thomas Collins,* Edinburgh, 1809.

PLATE 45

Bishop Walburga's cathedral, Our Lady of the Evening, was the only church in Wein-am-Rhein. "The Bish," as he was known throughout his diocese, welcomed everyone into "God's Tavern," and a bucket brigade was formed from the wine cellar to the nave. The ensuing Celebration of Bacchus raged all through the night, and reached depths of drunken abandon perhaps unequaled in the annals of Western debauchery.

PLATE 46

Our Lady of the Evening on the following day. Although this is, of course, a modern photograph, the appearance of the cathedral is exactly the same as it was on the morning of the first of May 1807, since the Papal bull that excommunicated Bishop Walburga also decreed that the church be preserved, unchanged, as an enduring reminder of the results of "reckless secularization of Holy wine holdings."[1]

P. D. Q., of course, had been excommunicated long before, at the same time that he was declared a cardinal sin, but the possibility that the devastation wrought upon the town's only cathedral might conceivably be regarded in certain circles as a direct result of his music made him fear for his physical safety in Wein-am-Rhein. The worst days of the Inquisition were over, but Rome still had its ways, and P. D. Q. had often wondered about the two strangers with Italian accents who had been hanging around off and on ever since the performance, several years earlier, of his *Missa Hilarious*. And so, on the night of the morning after what may have been history's most ephemeral concert, suffering from what may have been history's most enduring hangover, P. D. Q. Bach left town in a hurry for the last time in his life, thus bringing the Soused Period to a fitting close.

[1] Eventually, through some adroit political maneuvering, the Bishop managed to get himself not only reinstated into the Church, but canonized as well, and the night of P. D. Q. Bach's memorable concert is still called *Walpurgisnacht* in German-speaking countries.

PLATE 47

Faced with the necessity of exiling himself (temporarily, he must have thought), P. D. Q. chose a town that he had visited in very similar circumstances fifty-two years before, when he and Zahnstocher had fled Dudeldorf after the disastrous incident involving Prince Ferdinand (see page 7). P. D. Q. had nothing but fond memories of Baden-Baden-Baden,[1] and since he was now a wealthy man and could afford to live in the same high style which Prince Ferdinand's appropriated purse had made possible on the previous visit, he rather looked forward to a change of scene.

[1] shown here as it looked after it was rebuilt following the celebration of P. D. Q. Bach's death.

PLATE 48

Unfortunately, this time his reputation had preceded him, and Baden-Baden-Baden was no Wein-am-Rhein; as soon as news of his arrival got around town, 90 percent of the population moved out. Plagued by the resulting loneliness, and by an inability to sleep due to the epochal hangover still throbbing in his head, P. D. Q. whiled away the time by writing a continuous succession of pieces, proceeding from one to the next virtually without stopping, except occasionally to scratch. There is no doubt that P. D. Q., usually so slothlike, was writing music simply to keep his mind off his mind; the only part of his stay in Baden-Baden-Baden that he could actually be said to have enjoyed was a surprise visit from one of his few friendly relatives.

PLATE 49

Betty-Sue Bach in 1807 was not the same lass she had been in 1766, but then again, neither was P. D. Q. She obviously shared his love of food and drink, and he was glad to see her when she arrived in Baden-Baden-Baden, even though he was in no shape to do the things that were what he liked her for. Betty-Sue had been vacationing in Freiburg, intending later in the month to visit P. D. Q. in Wein-am-Rhein; but when the stream of refugees from Baden-Baden-Baden began to flow into Freiburg, the reason for their uprooting quickly became known all over town; as soon as she heard about P. D. Q.'s new whereabouts, Betty-Sue hurried to his floor-side, and not a moment too soon. For on the day after her arrival, at exactly eleven o'clock in the evening, May 5, 1807, P. D. Q. leaned over to Betty-Sue and said in a hoarse whisper, "Time, gentlemen." With these closing words, "the walking pub," as he used to be called in London, fell back and, at the age of sixty-five, exchanged this world for the next.

PLATE 50

Since P. D. Q. was a wealthy man when he died, Betty-Sue arranged for him to be buried in a sumptuous mausoleum on the outskirts of Baden-Baden-Baden, and it was on this tomb that the controversial dates 1807-1742 were inscribed, along with an epitaph presumably composed by the local doggerel-catcher:[1]

> *Hier liegt ein Mann ganz ohnegleich;*
> *Im Leibe dick, an Sünden reich.*
> *Wir haben ihn in das Grab gesteckt,*
> *Weil es uns dünkt er sei verreckt.*

> Here lies a man with sundry flaws
> And numerous sins upon his head;
> We buried him today because
> As far as we can tell, he's dead.

Eventually P. D. Q. Bach's family was successful in having him moved to an unmarked pauper's grave; the mausoleum was destroyed in the 1840's (with the open approval of Wilhelm Friedrich Ernst Bach, the last male descendant of Johann Sebastian) by a wrecking crew under the direction of Felix Mendelssohn. Fortunately for posterity, several detailed pictures of it have survived.

---

[1] It was the duty of this minor official to compose short poems and set them to music as rounds, or (as the English called them) catches.

PLATE 51

As soon as P. D. Q. Bach's obituary was printed in the local newspaper, everybody moved back into town, and life returned to normal in Baden-Baden-Baden.

PLATE 52

In spite of P. D. Q. Bach's timely death, Betty-Sue did go to Wein-am-Rhein and, as has been mentioned earlier, ended up marrying one of P. D. Q.'s staunchest drinking companions, Jonathan "Boozey" Hawkes. But she never forgot P. D. Q., and years later in Liverpool, when the news reached her concerning the Bach family's removal of the body from the mausoleum and the defacement of the inscriptions thereon, Betty-Sue sent some money to an artist her husband had known in Wein-am-Rhein, requesting him to erect a suitable monument to the memory of her cousin. The monument still stands, and on its plaque one may still read the poem that "Boozey" and Betty-Sue wrote in memory of history's strangest composer:

> He lies in death, as lie he did in life,
> Oblivious to worldly cares and strife;
> No base distractions rile his sodden brain,
> And odious Ambition waits in vain
> For him to rise; sweet Gabriel, play on!
> You'll nothing rouse, except perhaps a yawn;
> For P. D. Q. will waken when he will,
> And even God must wait that day until.

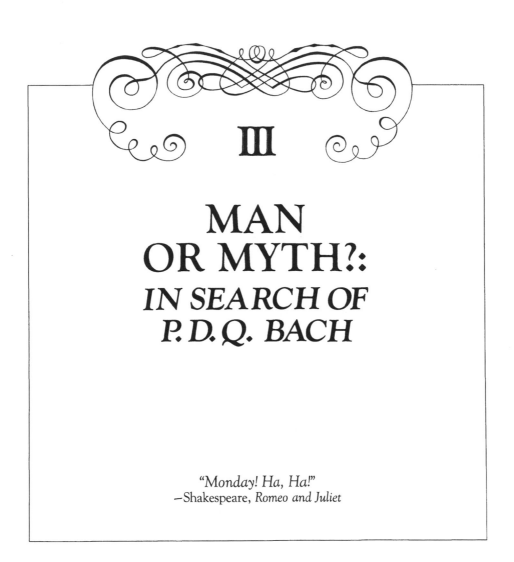

III

MAN
OR MYTH?:
IN SEARCH OF
P. D. Q. BACH

"Monday! Ha, Ha!"
—Shakespeare, *Romeo and Juliet*

Since the investigative methods employed by the author in researching P. D. Q. Bach and his music differ in many respects quite markedly from those used by other scholars in dealing with Mozart and Haydn and all the lesser but nevertheless competent composers that dotted the musical landscape of the Age of Enlightenment, it has seemed more than likely that the reader would find a brief treatment of this interesting area of no little interest. This section, therefore, deals with four interrelated subjects: (1) the actual discovery of manuscripts and other material; (2) the University of Southern North Dakota at Hoople, whose support, however unwilling (the author was given tenure before the dean—or even the head of the music department—had heard any of P. D. Q. Bach's music, and the numerous attempts at terminating the author's contract in spite of his tenure have been thwarted by an unusually militant chapter of the American Association of University Professors[1] under the leadership of Prof. Sven "Chainsaw" Swenson), has been of inestimable value, especially in that it serves to bring the author together with those few dedicated students who are willing to brave the slings and arrows of outrageous fortune cookies hurled at them by the Davids and William Tells among their peers and superiors; (3) the tracing of the descendants of P. D. Q. and his cousin[2] Betty-Sue Bach, the illegitimate status of whose sexual union makes genealogical inquiry particularly difficult; (4) miscellaneous manuscripts, including sketches, unfinished works, attempts at engraving, and other material whose biographical interest makes up for its more than usually slight musical value.

It is hoped that after ingesting these morsels of information the reader will feel satiated, at the very least, concerning the most misunderstanding composer ever to blemish the smorgasbord of musical history.

[1] A.A.U.P.

[2] actually first cousin once removed.

The discovery by the author of P. D. Q. Bach's oratorio The
Seasonings *on December 11, 1965, behind a restaurant in
Kandern, Germany, on the edge of the Black Forest.*

Three years later, almost to the day, the two madrigals from The Triumphs of Thusnelda *were found in a vacant lot on the outskirts of London. The author, smarting from published comments alleging a facial similarity between himself and P. D. Q., has grown a beard.*

The radio program Report from Hoople, an early attempt to bring the music of P. D. Q. Bach before the public, was curtailed in 1967 by the FCC.

It has become a tradition for the author to play the role of P. D. Q. Bach in the Potion Play, a dramatization of P. D. Q.'s life presented every ten years by selected students and townspeople of Hoople.

A "publicity shot" for the second concert of P. D. Q. Bach's music in Philadelphia, one of the main citadels of American musical culture.

The concert itself was not as well attended as the first had been. One of the reviews mentioned "long lines at the box office," but in all fairness it must be admitted that the lines consisted of people demanding refunds.

The University of Southern North Dakota at Hoople, looking south across the campus.

Another view.

The Science Building.

The Fine Arts Building.

The School of Agriculture and Drama, with the Administration Building on the right.

Most of the students live at home and commute to campus; a few, however, live in Loft Hall, a rustic but comfortable dormitory.

The author arriving for a heavy day of classes, both of which are held in the North Wing of the Henry A. Wallace Memorial Sty. The building in the background is the State Reformatory for Young Hussies and Trollops.

Newly discovered choral works are usually first performed by the Pals of Orpheus, a glee club formed by combining the barbershop quartet, the Calico Cats, with the Gingham Dogs, a female vocal trio.

In the beginning, the author's search for P. D. Q. Bach manuscripts was a lonely one. Now, however, he often goes on expeditions with the members of his graduate seminar in "Originality Through Incompetence," an in-depth study of P. D. Q.'s style; this has the twofold advantage of easing his own burden and at the same time providing his students with a highly educational experience. The pictures on the following four pages document the discovery, at the actual site of the eighteenth-century town of Wein-am-Rhein, of the Toot Suite for calliope four hands.

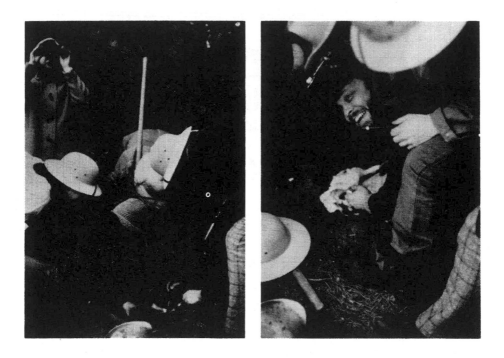

Historically speaking, there is no doubt that the most important breakthrough in P. D. Q. Bachiography during the last few years has been the locating of P. D. Q.'s final resting place, the unmarked pauper's grave to which he was moved by his relatives. Taking a tip from the Black Forest legend which says that the patch of ground where P. D. Q. Bach was buried grows the best wine grapes in all of Europe, the author and his students, after weeks of wine-tasting cruises up and down the Rhine, discovered this simple, unidentified grave on a gentle slope approximately halfway between Wein-am-Rhein and the neighboring town of Glug. On the night of the 31st of October 1974, the coffin was dug up and opened, and even if the various scientific tests to which the skeleton was later subjected had not provided ample proof of the identity of the corpse, the fact that the left hand was clutching a beer stein and the right hand a sheet of music paper would seem to be sufficient evidence to any but the most closed-minded pedant. (Photograph of the grave and the author's thumb by the author.)

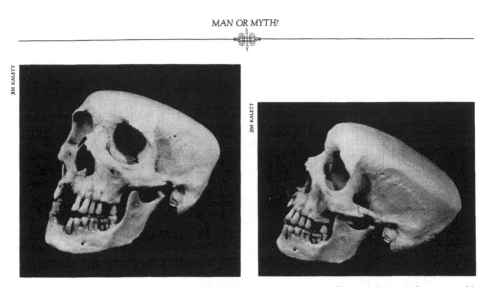

Two views of P. D. Q. Bach's remarkable skull. The truly impressive smallness of the cranial cavity could, according to anatomical experts, very well have had some bearing on P. D. Q.'s musical thinking. An examination of the skull's inner surfaces has revealed that the hangover that plagued P. D. Q. during the entire contrition period was so extraordinarily tenacious that it lasted well after P. D. Q.'s death. In fact, he may still have it; tests using the new alcohol-dating technique indicate that the hangover could have a half-life of as long as a hundred and forty years.

Many of the descendants of P. D. Q. and Betty-Sue have proven to be untraceable, due in large part, no doubt, to calculated name-changing and other forms of obfuscation. Several, however, have been definitely identified, and several others are caught in the glare of circumstantial but compelling evidence.

One of P. D. Q.'s grandchildren was Sir Edmund Bach, who made the first descent of the Matterhorn.

*Sir Edmund's second son, Zwei Bach, emigrated to the United
States, where he fought on at least one side of the Civil War
and earned the nickname "Old Ironstomach."*

Balder Bach was a clerk in a Hamburg Homburg factory who spent his spare time pouring ink on the streets.

Damon "Dimmy" Bach retains his position as a doorman at a Liverpool hotel that has been closed for thirteen years. He refuses to discuss the subject of his ancestry.

After being given a bottle of alcoholic spirits "Sneaky" Pete Bog admitted that his parents had spelled their last name "Bach." He also admitted that he set the Reichstag fire, signed the Declaration of Independence, and won twenty-five gold medals at the Tokyo Olympics.

"Sneaky" Pete pointed out his rich uncle, who he said had changed his name, although he didn't know to what. Although the author "tailed" the man for several hours and was able to photograph him five times, no one who has seen the pictures has been able to identify him.

Brock Bock is a publicity agent for a New York theatrical concern. The author's encounter with him was photographed from the other side of the street by a student.

When asked whether he or his family had changed the spelling of his last name, Mr. Bock became less than cordial.

(142)

The author, by no means unfamiliar with this type of reaction to his questions, tried to remain in good spirits.

Having successfully avoided answering the author's questions, Mr. Bock, obviously a suspicious sort, spotted the photographer just before the latter was run over by a bus.

(143)

The only fully established living descendant of P. D. Q. found by the author was Brunhilde Bach, known to her friends as "Bébé." Far from being ashamed of her ancestry, "Bébé" Bach actually modeled her life upon that of P. D. Q.; she drank and ate and played the piano exactly as he had two centuries earlier. Unfortunately she did not inherit his constitution, and shortly after this photograph was taken she died at the age of twenty-nine.

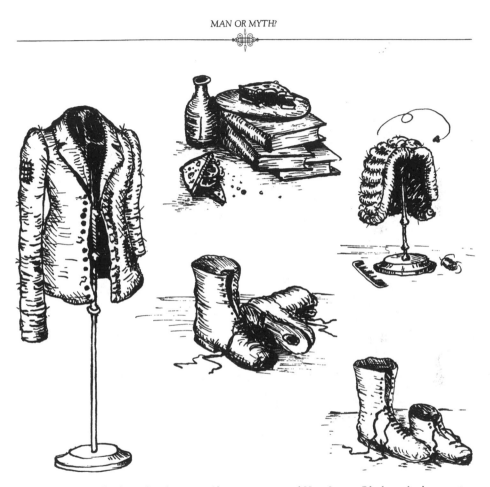

One of P. D. Q. Bach's closest friends was an Alsatian artist named Hans-Jacques Pferdemerde; the page, in a 1780 sketchbook, on which these drawings occur is inscribed "chez le komponist P. D. Q. Bach, en attendant ihnen venir à" ("at the home of the composer P. D. Q. Bach, waiting for him to come to").

A page from one of P. D. Q.'s extremely rare sketchbooks, showing the opening of Iphigenia in Brooklyn, the names of several female acquaintances, a shopping list, and some thematic ideas he evidently thought were not worth working on (the note at the lower right, "I must finish this piece," was apparently not heeded). It also shows how he felt about his brother Johann Christian and how he cheated at tic-tac-toe.

(146)

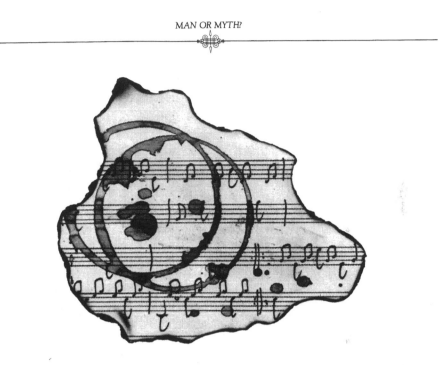

A fragment of the "Andre Gigue" from The Notebook for Betty-Sue Bach, showing the ring-marks left on the manuscript paper by P. D. Q.'s beer stein. This kind of mark, which P. D. Q. called a "Ring des Nibelungen" after his favorite brand of beer, has aided considerably in the authentication and dating of many P. D. Q. manuscripts.

The beginning of another piece from the Notebook for Betty-Sue Bach, *from the "Edsel" sketchbook. Donated to the P. D. Q. Bach Museum at the University of Southern North Dakota at Hoople by the Ford Foundation.*

An unfinished keyboard piece employing invertible counterpoint.

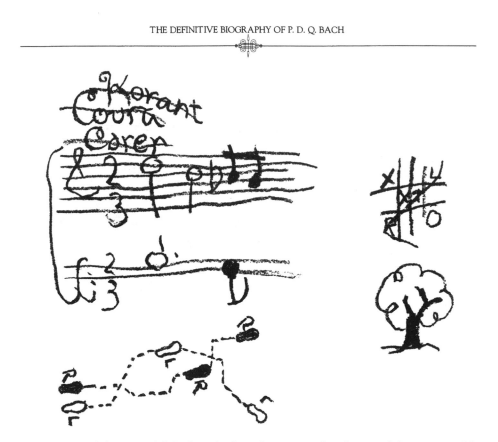

During the Initial Plunge period P. D. Q. tried to learn the steps as well as the musical characteristics of the various Baroque dances.

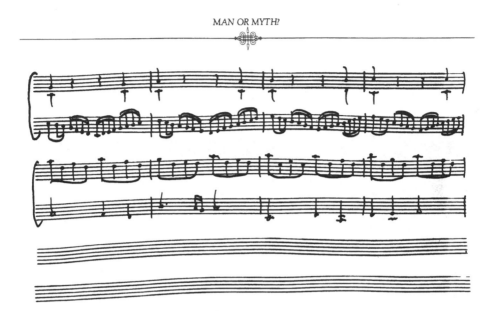

P. D. Q.'s plagiarism took many forms, some more subtle than others. If this fragment of an unfinished piano sonata is turned upside down and held in front of a mirror, it will be seen to be identical to the first eight measures of Mozart's famous C-major sonata.

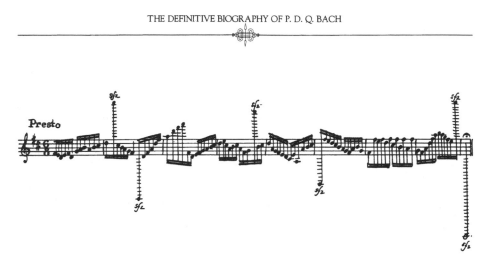

Presto

Around 1800 one of Wein-am-Rhein's most interesting residents, a mystic false teeth manufacturer who called himself Doktor Schmerzlos, commissioned P. D. Q. to write an ambitious work for piano entitled Trance and Dental Etudes; Book I was to be for the right hand alone, and Book II for the left hand. P. D. Q. made some desultory sketches for the piece, but never completed it, since in 1801 Doktor Schmerzlos died, rendering the commissioning fee uncollectible.

The Trance and Dental Etudes *were evidently intended for performance on the* Überklavier *(superpiano) invented in 1797 by Klarck Känt, a Munich piano maker who must have demonstrated the new instrument to P. D. Q. on one of the latter's business trips. It had a range of over fifteen octaves, but its use, unlike its keyboard, was never widespread.*

P. D. Q.'s attempts at engraving the pieces shown on this and the next three pages were even more disastrous than his attempts at composing them.

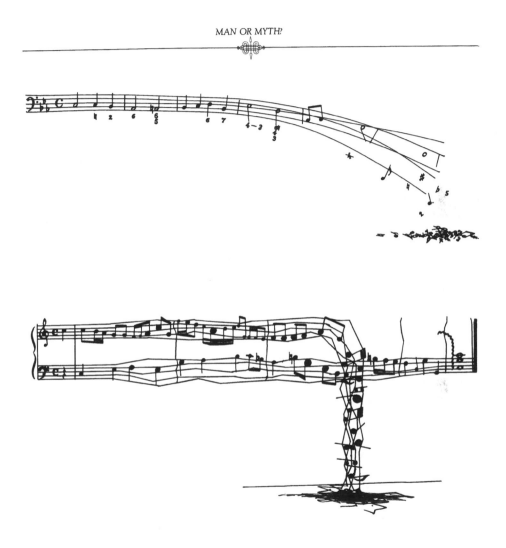

II

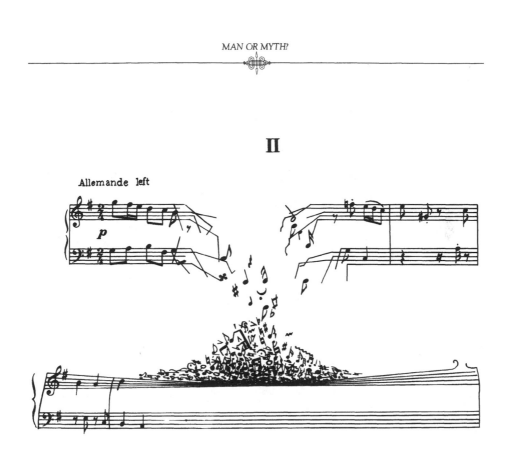

Toward the end of his life P. D. Q. became very frugal; this attempt to write an entire piano sonata on one page of manuscript paper has yet to be deciphered.

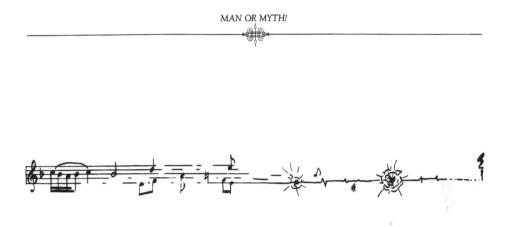

Unlike Mozart's Requiem *and Bartok's* Third Piano Concerto, *the piece that P. D. Q. Bach was working on when he died has never been finished by anyone else.*

Hans-Jacques Pferdemerde designed this book plate as a present to P. D. Q., who, since he never read books, used it as a coaster.

MAN OR MYTH?

IV

"SUCH A HORRID CLANG":
AN ANNOTATED CATALOGUE OF THE MUSIC OF P.D.Q. BACH

"Always use new rubbers."
—Fannie W. Farmer, *The Boston Cooking-School Cook Book*

P. D. Q. Bach, like Mozart and Fats Waller, did not affix opus numbers to his compositions; the present author, therefore, has assumed the responsibility of cataloguing the works, and the number in parentheses after the title of each work is its Schickele number. Since the scantiness of our information about P. D. Q. precludes arranging the pieces in any consistent chronological order, the numbers have been assigned on the basis of intrinsic rather than temporal considerations; within each creative period the listing is simply in the order of discovery.

The numbers in parentheses after the key or instrumentation of many of the works, e.g. (rec. 2&5), refer to the recordings as listed in the Discography.

Those who feel that performing the music of P. D. Q. Bach, like taking cold showers and drinking raw eggs, builds character, will be interested in knowing that due to a colossal misunderstanding most of the pieces are available in printed form, either by purchase or on rental, from Theodore Presser Co., Bryn Mawr, Pennsylvania 19010; a brochure will be sent by the publisher upon request.

THE INITIAL PLUNGE

THE Initial Plunge was the period during which P. D. Q. Bach learned all that he ever learned about the craft of musical composition; it lasted about six days. The pieces written during this period indicate that P. D. Q. did not study with anyone in Vienna, where he was living at the time; the Initial Plunge works that have been discovered are modeled upon the music that P. D. Q. had heard when he was a boy in Leipzig: the music of Vivaldi, Telemann, and above all, his own father. He must have realized that this style was hopelessly out of fashion in 1777, but he may have reasoned that if it should happen to come back into fashion, he would be the first to cash in on it.

In all likelihood P. D. Q.'s first compositional effort was the *Neo-Trio Sonata* he showed to Padre Martini in Wein-am-Rhein. Although the manuscript has been lost, the Italian master's description of it[1] survives, from which we can deduce that the piece was a remarkable tribute to the inexperience of its composer.

[1] which is quoted out of context somewhere else in the book.

TRAUMAREI
for unaccompanied piano (S. 13)
D minor (rec. 3)

The *Traumarei* exists in two different forms, the later of which is part of the *Notebook for Betty-Sue Bach*,[1] but it is properly dealt with here because it was first discovered separately and because it is the only piece in the *Notebook* that was written during the Initial Plunge. Of the three extant pieces from this period, the *Traumarei* is the least ambitious, and therefore, the most successful. It is a slow, introspective work; occasional outbursts of rapid scale passages alternate with aimless meanderings, as if the composer had written it while sitting at the piano one cold winter night, musing over some past nightmare, distant but not forgotten. The temptation to identify the trauma of the title with the death of the composer's father when P. D. Q. was eight years old is irresistible, which is more than can be said for the piece itself; as the work of a rank amateur, however, it at least has the virtue of humility, in that it pretends to be no more than what it is: rank and amateurish.

The author of the present treatise had the good fortune, on one of his manuscript-hunting tours of Europe, to stumble across the actual piano owned by P. D. Q. Bach during the Initial Plunge; the resulting sprained ankle is regarded by the author as a small price to pay for such an important find, for the Furtfurt piano answers a question that had been nagging P. D. Q. Bach scholars ever since the discovery of the *Traumarei*: why, since the piece is definitely in the Baroque style and not the Classical, was the *Traumarei* written for piano and not harpsichord? Although the pianoforte,[2] with its characteristic hammer action (as opposed to the equally characteristic plucking action of the harpsichord), was invented early in the eighteenth century, it did not begin to overshadow the harpsichord until the last quarter of that century, and Baroque works written expressly for the piano are rare indeed, although not as rare as Romantic works written expressly for the krummhorn. Was P. D. Q. writing for what he, in a moment of uncharacteristic clear-sightedness, perceived to be the wave of the future, or was he simply writing for what happened to be at hand?

The answer to this question is as misleading as the question itself. Upon hearing the piano,[3] we are struck by the realization that P. D. Q. did not compromise as much as we had thought, for even allowing for almost two hundred years of inadequate care (the present owner, Herr Heinrich Seifenblase, uses the strings for slicing eggs and grating

---

[1] q.v. if interested; otherwise q.n.v.

[2] not to be confused with panforte, a kind of Italian fruit and nut cake which, though it lacks the range and versatility of the pianoforte, is considerably better tasting.

[3] which those of a scholarly and/or masochistic bent may do on the recording indicated above.

cheese; repeated attempts to persuade the musicology department at the U. of S.N.D. at H. to purchase the piano have been repeatedly rebuffed by a certain professor who shall remain nameless),[1] the

---

[1] Put that in your pipe and smoke it, Dr. Johansen!

tone of the Furtfurt piano is resoundingly tinny; in fact its timbre may perhaps be best described as an almost uncanny combination of harpsichord and kazoo.

ECHO SONATA
for Two Unfriendly Groups of Instruments (S. 99999999)
F Major; flute, oboe, bassoon,
horn, trumpet, trombone (rec. 3)

In this work P. D. Q. demonstrates his inability to handle the antiphonal concept, a concept so central to the structure of Baroque instrumental music that P. D. Q. could no more ignore it than understand it. The musical statements made by the woodwinds, if taken alone, would seem to indicate a giant step forward for the neophyte Bach, since they are surprisingly well conceived when compared to the clumsy vagaries of the *Traumarei*; however, the answers to these statements, played by the brasses, immediately erase any overly optimistic expectations the listener may have developed during the first four measures. It is perhaps worth our while to look at this piece in some detail, and in the process, it is to be hoped, gain some insight into P. D. Q. Bach's personality.

The opening statement by the woodwinds, one of the most felicitous ever penned by the not-so-young Bach, is answered by the brasses in a most rude fashion, twisting the woodwinds' simple smile into a diabolical grimace. The woodwinds valiantly continue without losing their composure, to be answered this time with absolute silence in the brasses. Although it is equally antipathetic to the spirit of exchange inherent in the term "echo sonata," silence is nevertheless better than mockery, so the woodwinds pull themselves together and, like a band of pilgrims marching to the Holy Land, resume their journey with humility, keeping their eyes fixed upon their destination, and ignoring the now increasingly constant heckling from the Philistine brasses. Seeing that their insults have no effect, the brasses become tired of their sport and decide to play along with the chaste woodwinds. They even begin to answer the pilgrims respectfully, and for a time it seems as if they may actually join those whom they so recently jeered, but no—they are drowsy, exhausted by their crude antics, and their conversation becomes more and more halting, until finally they fall by the wayside, sound asleep. This, however, will not do, for this is after all an echo sonata, and the piece cannot very well be finished without them; yet it is not until the exasperated woodwinds threaten to employ the most extreme forms of physical coercion that the soporific brasses grudgingly play the last chord.

One is tempted to speculate that the two instrumental groups in the *Echo Sonata* represented to P. D. Q. Bach two opposing aspects of his own personality,[1] and in this light it is interesting to note that it is the vulgar brasses, and not the civilized woodwinds, who have the last word. This work, in fact, may be viewed as a sort of musical *Mein Kampf*, a blueprint for future outrages which, although certainly innocuous compared to those perpetrated by that later scourge of Europe, would nevertheless probably have been prevented had people realized what they were letting themselves in for.

---

[1] One of the strongest supporters of this line of reasoning was Florestan Schumann, whose article "Notes & Neuroses" in the Feb. 1854 issue of the *Neue Zeitschrift für Musik* was gently rebutted in the following issue by an article entitled "Turn Off Your Mind, Relax, Float Down the Rhine," contributed anonymously but suspected to be the work of a distant relative, Eusebius Schumann.

GROSS CONCERTO
for Divers Flutes, Two Trumpets, and Strings (S. −2)
C major.
Majestätisch—mit einer schnellen Mässigkeit—unglaublich majestätisch
Langsam aber zart
Schnell; keine Mässigkeit

The *Gross Concerto* is the magnum opus of the Initial Plunge, if that is not a contradiction in terms. It is, as its catalogue number indicates, still a very early work, but it is significant in two ways: it was P. D. Q.'s first orchestral work, and it was the first work in which he wrote for instruments that other composers had either no knowledge of or the good sense to avoid.

The term "Divers" in the title does not, of course, refer to any submarine activity; it is rather an archaic spelling of the word "diverse," and diverse indeed are the flutes played by the soloist in this concerto. The instruments are illustrated below; suffice it to say here that were it not for P. D. Q. Bach, the literature for the left-handed sewer flute and the Oscar Mayer wiener whistle would not be what it is today.

The first movement, Majestically—with a fast moderateness—unbelievably majestically, is followed by the second movement, Slow but tender; the virtuously short last movement, Fast; no moderateness, brings up the rear.

It will be remembered that this work was written for and first played by the miniature flautist "Peeping" Tom Pollex; with the benefit of hindsight we can see that P. D. Q. was extremely fortunate in having a real virtuoso as an interpreter. Pollex's performance was so dazzling that no one in the audience seemed to notice, or at any rate care about, the painfully awkward passages that abound in the piece. Professor Lewissohn Clark, of Northwestern University, has written extensively about one of these, the famous "Northwestern Passage"; it occurs near the end of the middle movement, and in it P. D. Q. spends two very long measures building toward a cadence that he never achieves, after which he simply retraces his steps back to where he started and goes off in another direction. Weaknesses such as this would certainly not have escaped the attention of Prince Fred's sophisticated friends had not the overwhelming showmanship of Thomas Pollex blinded their ears.

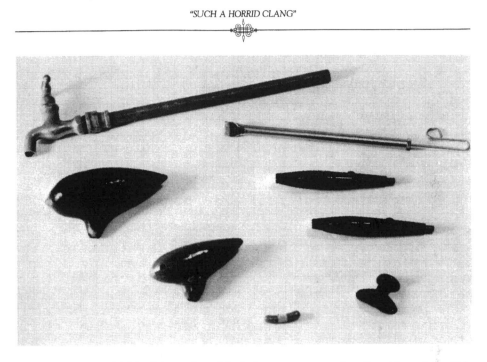

Clockwise from upper left: left-handed sewer flute, slide whistle, two tonettes, nose flute, Oscar Mayer wiener whistle, ocarina, grosse ocarina.

2
THE SOUSED PERIOD

T HE Soused Period was by far the longest period in P. D. Q. Bach's creative
life, lasting from the beginning of 1778
until the end of April 1807. During this period
P. D. Q. developed a richer sense of harmony due
to almost constant double vision, and began to exhibit the symptoms of juvenile senility that were to
characterize the bulk of his mature output. His style
underwent an abrupt change after the *Gross Concerto*; as soon as he settled in Wein-am-Rhein after
that historic premiere he began to write in the more
up-to-date style of Haydn and Mozart,[1] not without, however, occasional stylistic backtrackings
which may be interpreted as premonitions of the
earlier style of his last period.

---

[1] and all the lesser but nevertheless competent composers
that dotted the musical landscape of the Age of Enlightenment.

CONCERTO FOR HORN AND HARDART (S. 27)
B♭ major; chamber orchestra. (rec. 1&5)

Allegro con brillo
Tema con variazione
Menuetto con panna e zucchero

The influence of classical music upon the modern commercial world is far from far-reaching, which makes even more remarkable the fact that a chain of automat restaurants should be named after a concerto by an eighteenth-century German composer whose best-known quality is his obscurity. It seems safe to say that most of the people who frequent the Horn & Hardart restaurants in New York and other cities do not realize that they are indirectly paying homage to a long- and deservedly-dead composer; such are the ironies of art.

The hardart is one of the most bizarre instruments for which P. D. Q. Bach wrote. Its origins are unclear, but the reasons for its demise are painfully evident to anyone who has heard this concerto; in fact, there is not a single eighteenth-century hardart in existence today (the one played by this author in his performances of the concerto was reconstructed from eighteenth-century descriptions of the instrument by craftsmen at the Obsolete Instruments Department of the U. of S.N.D. at H.). It has a range of over two almost chromatic octaves, with each successive tone possessing a different quality or timbre. The sound-producing devices include a plucked string, bottles which are blown and struck, a bicycle horn, various whistles, and a cooking timer. Windows in the center section, which can be opened after inserting the necessary coins in the slots, contain the different mallets required to play the percussion components, as well as sandwiches and pieces of pie, which are particularly welcome during long concerts. A spigot on the front serves coffee; above it is painted the inscription MINOR LABOR MATRIS (Less Work for Mother). The balloons which are burst at the end of the concerto with an ice pick and a shotgun add a festive touch. Due to its unusual length (over nine feet) and the great variety of motions necessary to produce its tones, the hardart requires of its player a considerable amount of athletic as well as musical ability.

The first movement (Cheerfully with brillo) is one of your typical sonata-form movements, with the truncated recapitulation one has come to expect from history's laziest composer. Formally speaking, the second movement (Theme with variations) is unusual in that the variations are not variations of that theme; they seem to be variations of some other theme. Having been employed almost exclusively as a single-line instrument up until now, the hardart finally gets a chance to display its chordal abilities in the last movement (Minuet with cream and sugar).

The catalogue number of the concerto may, at first glance, seem to be arbitrary; upon reflection, however, it will become obvious that it is the product of multiplying the square root of the sum of the number of sound-producing devices on the hardart and the number of letters in the composer's name by the number of movements in the piece.

SINFONIA CONCERTANTE (S. 98.6)
D major; lute, balalaika, double reed slide music stand, ocarina, left-handed sewer flute, bagpipes, and strings. (rec. 1)

Sehr unruhig mit schmalz
Andante senza moto
Presto nicht schleppend

The *Sinfonia Concertante*, one of the most normal of P. D. Q. Bach's works, is also a striking example of the Soused Period's most characteristic characteristic: a sense of orchestration and tonal color so exotic that it borders on the irresponsible. It is hard to imagine, for instance, two instruments more unevenly matched than the lute and the bagpipes. The balalaika adds international flavor and very little else, which is more than can be said for the ocarina, or sweet potato, as it has euphemistically come to be called. The left-handed sewer flute and the double reed slide music stand were not uncommon in the eighteenth century—both Bach and Handel were quite familiar with them, which is why the repertoire for these instruments does not include anything by Bach and Handel—but P. D. Q. Bach was, as far as we know, the only composer with enough daring and ignorance to write for both simultaneously, using their incompatibility as a structural element in the composition.

The manuscript of the *Sinfonia Concertante* was discovered by the author at the bottom of a closet in the McEisenstadt castle in Scotland, where it had

Double reed slide music stand.

lain apparently untouched since Morrie MacEisenstadt (pictured below), an execrable early-nineteenth-century piper who had been forbidden, on pain of death, to play the great *piobaireachd* litera-ture for that instrument, acquired it for his own personal use, presumably from "Boozey" Hawkes in Liverpool.

PERVERTIMENTO
for Bagpipes, Bicycle, and Balloons (S. 66)
G major; strings. (rec. 2)

Allegro moulto
Romanza II (Adagio sireno)
Minaret and Trio
Romanza I (Chi largo)
Presto changio

Since the discovery of the *Pervertimento*, even his detractors have had to admit that P. D. Q. Bach must be considered history's greatest late-eighteenth-century Southern German composer of multi-movement works for bagpipes and chamber orchestra. Probably with the encouragement of Thomas Collins, the perverted piper for whom the piece was penned, P. D. Q. used the instrument in a great variety of ways, some of which are regarded as improper, if not downright immoral, by most pipers today. To these purists the only thing worse than detaching the melody chanter (pipe) and playing it alone as if it were an oboe is detaching the drones and playing them in the same manner, and the use in the penultimate movement of the practice chanter—usually taken out only in private, behind locked doors—is particularly offensive to modern tastes. Thomas Collins' attitude, however, was "If it feels good, play it," and even the most sensitive listener will agree that in point of fact the *Pervertimento* is no more abnormal or unnatural than any other work by the same composer.

It is common knowledge that P. D. Q. invented a technique for playing arpeggios (broken chords) on the foot pedals of an organ; the technique, known as the "tootsie roll," is now standard practice among organists, and obviously this inventiveness with pedal technique stood P. D. Q. in good stead when it came to writing for the bicycle. Most people do not realize that the bicycle was originally invented as a musical instrument, and that only in the nineteenth century, when composers began to ignore it in favor of the saxophone, did it gradually come to be regarded as a vehicle. P. D. Q. apparently played the bicycle himself, and judging by the solo part in the *Pervertimento*, he must have been quite adept; the siren song in the second movement requires a high degree of pedal control, since any variation in speed results in a corresponding variation in pitch (see photograph below).

The writing for balloons is, as one might expect, in the typical French style of the day. Balloons had been invented in France for an entirely different purpose, but French musicians (or *musiciens français*, as they liked to call themselves) were quick to realize that balloons had unique expressive possibilities, and by the middle of the eighteenth century the Paris school of composers was known throughout Europe for colorful balloon writing.

The numbering of the second and fourth movements seems puzzling until one remembers that P. D. Q. never numbered his pages, a fact that must be taken into consideration when analyzing the formal construction of many of his pieces.

SERENUDE
for devious instruments (S. 36·24·36)
D major; 2 kazoos, 2 slide whistles, tromboon,
windbreaker & slide windbreaker, shower hose
in D, and strings.

Shake allegro
Andante alighieri
Four-voice frugue

The *Serenude*, like the *Sinfonia Concertante*, is ac-tually a cross between the late-eighteenth-century serenade and the early-eighteenth-century concerto grosso, employing as it does a whole raft of unusual solo instruments. P. D. Q. used these same instruments in his oratorio *The Seasonings*, evidently hoping against hope that the addition of voices would make them sound better. More experienced composers could have told him, had they been on speaking terms with him, that any attempt to make the instruments listed above sound better would be doomed to failure, although P. D. Q. probably wouldn't have listened to them anyway, since he wasn't on listening terms with them either.

The *Serenude* was first performed in the back room of the Sign of the Bull tavern in Wein-am-Rhein to an audience who couldn't tell the difference.

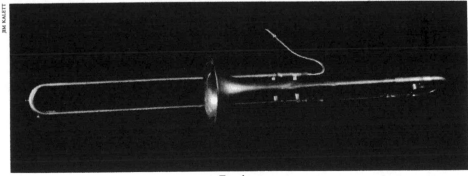

Tromboon.

PERÜCKENSTÜCK
(Hair Piece) from The Civilian Barber (S. 4F)
C major; soprano, pumpflute, double reed hookah in F, police trombone, and strings.

Although P. D. Q. Bach is known to have made quite a few sallies into the musical theater (see page 209), only two complete operas and fragments of a third, *The Civilian Barber*, have so far been recovered from oblivion. These fragments are tantalizing, because aside from what we can surmise from the text of the *Perückenstück* we know virtually nothing about even the plot of *The Civilian Barber*; the author has discovered the cast list reproduced below, but it seems to raise more questions than it answers:

The Count
The Countess
Le Figaro
A maid
A company of dragoons [1]
The King
The Queen
A doctor
Three chimney sweeps

[1] Dragoons are soldiers specially trained to quell disturbances in operas.

The ghost of Cleopatra
Marie Antoinette
Davy Crockett

The Civilian Barber first came to the author's attention when he ran across a loose sheet of manuscript paper containing sketches for the overture; in the margin is a note in P. D. Q.'s handwriting which, translated, reads: "Finish New Year's afternoon," indicating that the opera was premiered on the evening of January 1, probably toward the end of his life, since Davy Crockett was not born until 1786. The completed overture, however, has never been found, and in all honesty it must be admitted that the author of this book wrote an overture based upon the sketches and published it under his own name, without mentioning that of P. D. Q. Bach. In his defense, the author can only state that he was very young at the time, and that, had he known what P. D. Q.'s completed pieces sounded like, he would have stolen from somebody else.

SUITE
from The Civilian Barber (S. 4F)
**Various keys; 2 bassoons, 2 horns, 2 trumpets,
trombone, timpani, cellos, and basses.**

Entrance of the dragoons *(tempo di Marsha)*
Dance of St. Vitus
His Majesty's minuet
Fanfare for the royal shaft
Her Majesty's minuet
Departure of the dragoons *(tempo di on the double)*

This suite is a collection of instrumental pieces which were, one assumes, originally distributed throughout the opera. The manuscript was found lining the bottom of a birdcage tucked away in the basement of a house that once belonged to the Baden-Baden-Baden bandmaster; perhaps P. D. Q. had sent him the pieces in the hopes (evidently unfulfilled) of obtaining a performance at the bandshell in the local *Kurpark*.

The indication *tempo di Marsha* is either a misspelling of the common phrase *tempo di marcia* (march tempo) or a reference to the most peculiar soldier in the company, a fellow known to his barracks-mates as "Puff, the Magic Dragoon."

SCHLEPTET
in E♭ Major (S. 0)
E♭ major; flute, oboe, bassoon, horn, violin, viola,
and cello. (rec. 3 & 5)

Molto larghissimo—Allegro boffo
Menuetto con brio ma senza trio
Adagio saccarino
Yehudi menuetto
Presto hey nonny nonnio

This piece, written for seven of the most common instruments around, proves (if proof is necessary) that the excruciating *je ne sais quoi* of P. D. Q. Bach's Soused Period pieces cannot be blamed solely on the use of unrefined instruments such as the windbreaker and the left-handed sewer flute. The work is obviously a fairly late opus, since it is indebted (to put it kindly) to Beethoven's *Septet* in the same key. It is in five short movements, or, as P. D. Q. called them, shots; the last of these shows the influence of a band of gypsies by whom P. D. Q. was impressed, and, as he later discovered, robbed.

✥

THE STONED GUEST
a half-act opera (S. 86 proof)
C major; five characters, chamber orchestra. (rec. 4; 5 [excerpts])

CAST

DONNA RIBALDA, a high-born lady of the lowlands . . . . mezzanine soprano
CARMEN GHIA, a woman of ailing repute . . . . off-coloratura
DON OCTAVE, an itinerant nobleman . . . . bargain counter tenor
DOG, a large St. Bernard dog . . . . houndentenor
IL COMMENDATOREADOR, The Stoned Guest . . . . basso blotto

As was apparently the case with P. D. Q.'s other dramatic works, *The Stoned Guest* was first performed at the Howdyvolkstheater in Wein-am-Rhein; the initial reception was mixed, with tomatoes and eggs predominating. One of the most notable aspects of the opera is its large canine part (known in the eighteenth century as a *barcarolle*), which exceeds in virtuosity even the famous "Woofenpoof Song" from *Fido and Aeneas* by Arfenbach.

A synopsis of the plot follows:

Donna Ribalda finds herself lost in a forest after running away from a nocturnal attacker. She is joined, for no apparent reason, by Carmen Ghia. After the two singers take time out to brag about their careers, they express their woe by singing the famous duet "Woe." Upon hearing someone approaching, they decide that it would be safer if one of them disguised herself as a man. Donna Ribalda reluctantly volunteers and borrows a jacket from one of the orchestra

members. She then falls asleep on Carmen Ghia's lap as Don Octave enters and sings about the fact that he fails at everything he tries; that, indeed, singing octaves is the only thing he can do.

When Carmen Ghia asks him to take off his mask, which Don Octave had forgotten he had on, Donna Ribalda awakes and exclaims, "That's the villain who tried to abscond with me!" Don Octave is confused, since Donna Ribalda is disguised as a gentleman, but when she removes her jacket he realizes that she is his sister, a fact that Donna Ribalda also recognizes when Don Octave removes his mask. She scolds him for not even knowing his own house and for attacking his own sister, which he blames on drunkenness, but Carmen Ghia steps into this domestic argument, defending Don Octave and expressing her affection for him.

The animosity between the two women now breaks out in a contest to see who can sing the highest note and the longest note. Carmen Ghia wins on both counts, and she and Don Octave are just beginning to indulge in amorous play when Donna Ribalda re-

(183)

minds them that they are still lost, and points out that it is starting to snow, blow, and get dark. Don Octave's anguished cry, "Who can save us now?" is answered by the entrance of a large St. Bernard dog with a brandy cask around its neck, which turns out to be empty. Don Octave's pertinent question, "Now, who could have emptied it?" is answered by the entrance of the Stoned Guest himself, Il Commendatoreador, whose inebriated state limits his singing role to a mere six notes, after which he stands around staring at everyone.

The fevered anticlimax is reached as, in quick succession, Carmen Ghia admits that Il Commenda-

toreador is her father, Donna Ribalda strangles Carmen Ghia, Don Octave (attempting to avenge Carmen's death) accidentally stabs himself and expires, Il Commendatoreador draws a gun, shoots Donna Ribalda, and finally keels over dead drunk himself.

P. D. Q. originally intended to end the opera here, but the manager of the Howdyvolkstheater, Rudolfo Bingo, insisted on a happy ending, and so, after a poignant and refreshing pause, the dead bodies that are strewn around the stage suddenly and without explanation leap to their respective feet and sing a rousing finale.

TWO MADRIGALS
from The Triumphs of Thusnelda (S. 1601)
G minor & F major; soprano, mezzo-soprano,
counter tenor, tenor, bass (now published as SSATB).
(rec. 4; 5 [#2 only])

"The Queen to Me a Royal Pain Doth Give"
"My Bonnie Lass She Smelleth"

The two decades surrounding the year 1600 were heady years in England; not only was this the Golden Age of the English madrigal, but the same period also saw the flowering of English drama under Shakespeare, Marlowe and Jonson, and the deflowering of Queen Elizabeth under the Earl of Leicester.

During this time it was not uncommon for a number of pieces by different composers to be published together under a single title such as *The Triumphes of Oriana*, to name one of the most famous collections. It was this practice that inspired an eighteenth-century Norman nobleman, Count Pointercount, to launch a similar collection as a tribute to his wife Thusnelda, a singer who had recently triumphed over earthly cares by holding a high C so long that she died of asphyxiation. The project's hopes of success, however, grew dimmer and dimmer as, one by one, Europe's leading composers refused to contribute, each of them pointing out to the Count (with varying degrees of tact) that the madrigal had been dead as an art form for over a hundred years. Obviously, the only chance of

getting any pieces at all in the collection lay in finding a composer who was too dumb to know what was *au courant* and what was *passé*; thus it was that the sole contributor to *The Triumphs of Thusnelda* was P. D. Q. Bach.

Until recently the madrigals were assumed to be Contrition Period works, but the discovery in 1974 of Count Pointercount's diary has made it possible to establish that they were in fact composed in or before 1792, the year the Count took them back to Normandy with him, and after overcoming considerable opposition, managed to have them sung, as he put it, "over my wife's dead body."

The author, who also acted as editor, must in all fairness express his gratitude to the Theodore Presser Co. for publishing a modern performing edition of both madrigals, but he would be derelict in his duties if he did not also voice his violent disagreement with the decision to bowdlerize the texts, which, particularly in this day and age, seem hardly offensive. As a service, therefore, to those who may wish to perform these works with their original unadulterated words, the words, perhaps not so original but at any rate unadulterated, are printed below. It is suggested that in public performances the words be read aloud to the audience before they are sung, since in music of this type the different voices often sing the words at different times, resulting in a phenomenon known as "diction friction."

"The Queen to Me a Royal Pain Doth Give"

The Queen to me a royal pain doth give,
Yet were I so to say, I scarce would live
To see the fair Thusnelda once again.
Oy veh, oy veh (etc.)

A queen who reigns, yet keeps her powder dry,
Must power use where love would best apply
To keep me from Thusnelda once again.
Oy veh, oy veh (etc.)

Embedded on her throne, she would instead
Much rather be dethron'd upon her bed,
But once beneath the royal counterpane,
The ruler by her servant, Sleep, is slain,
And I to my Thusnelda fly again.
Oy veh, oy veh (etc.)

"My Bonnie Lass She Smelleth"

My bonnie lass she smelleth,
Making the flowers jealouth.
Fa la la (etc.)

My bonnie lass dismayeth
Me; all that she doth say ith:
Fa la la (etc.)

My bonnie lass she looketh like a jewel
And soundeth like a mule.
My bonnie lass she walketh like a doe
And talketh like a crow.
Fa la la (etc.)

My bonnie lass liketh to dance a lot;
She's Guinevere and I'm Sir Lancelot.[1]
Fa la la (etc.)

My bonnie lass I need not flatter;
What she doth not have doth not matter.
Oo la la (etc.)

My bonnie lass would be nice,
Yea, even at twice the price.
Fa la la (etc.)

[1] The meaning of this couplet is extinct; it was last seen in Scotland around the turn of the century.

CONCERTO FOR PIANO VS. ORCHESTRA (S. 88)
B♭ major.

Allegro immoderato
Andante con Mr. Moto
Vivace liberace

Some years ago, just as the Canadian pianist Glenn Gould and the New York Philharmonic Orchestra (as it was then called)[1] were about to begin playing one of the Brahms piano concertos, the conductor, Leonard Bernstein, turned around to the audience and publicly disassociated himself from the interpretation that was to follow. This inherent animosity between the conductor, representing the orchestra (i.e., the masses, the proletariat), and the soloist, representing only himself (i.e., the elite, one of the bosses), although well known to every musician, is usually kept below the surface, out of the audience's earsight. We have already seen, however, that one of the most thought-provoking, or at least provoking, characteristics of P. D. Q. Bach's

music is the almost twentieth-century way in which he expressly sets out to express the real realities that lie beyond the conventions of convention, and the *Concerto for Piano vs. Orchestra* is an exemplary example of this. During a recent performance, in fact, the contention between the two opposing forces manifested itself so physically that the house manager was forced to call the concerto on account of a cut above the conductor's left eye.

There was one occasion, on the other hand, when the work produced exactly the opposite effect: at its premiere performance in Wein-am-Rhein on the 1st of March 1807, the conductor *and* the pianist *and* the concertmaster, in an almost unheard-of display of unity, turned to the audience and disassociated themselves from the concerto itself.

[1] It still is.–Ed.

"EROTICA" VARIATIONS
for banned instruments and piano (S. 36EE)
Various keys. (rec. 6)

Theme: windbreaker
Variation I: balloons
Variation II: slide whistle
Variation III: slide windbreaker
Variation IV: lasso d'amore
Variation V: foghorn, bell, kazoo

In an article entitled "P. D. Q. Bach: Can It Happen Here?" appearing in the August 1973 issue of *The Musical Hindquarterly* (a publication of the A.M.J.),[1] Professor Paul Behrer argues that one of the reassuring reasons that a P. D. Q. Bach could not flourish in twentieth-century America is the existence now of quite stringent copyright laws, and certainly the lack of such laws in eighteenth-century Germany allowed that aspect of P. D. Q. Bach's style that has been called "manic plagiarism" to become developed to a degree that would be beyond the bounds of possibility in this day and age. As a general rule, the original passages in P. D. Q.'s music are due to his inability to remember how the piece that he was stealing from went.

In 1804 Immanuel Kant coined the phrase "absolute identity"; he invented the term not, as several modern philosophy textbooks state, to describe the soul's highest degree of self-knowledge, but rather to describe the relationship between the

theme of P. D. Q. Bach's *"Erotica" Variations* and that of Beethoven's *"Eroica" Variations*. The latter were written in 1802, which is probably when P. D. Q. heard them, although they are now referred to by the same name as the *Third Symphony*, which employs the same theme, but which Beethoven did not complete until 1804.[2]

Most of the instruments used in the *"Erotica" Variations* had been employed by P. D. Q. in other works, but the fourth variation introduces a new and unusually interesting instrument. Early in the eighteenth century, Viennese cowboys developed a technique of twirling their lariats over their heads with such great speed that a musical pitch was produced; by the end of the century the "lasso d'amore," as it came to be called, had been refined to the point of having a range of almost two octaves and a tone that Mozart called "weird," but the

[1] American Musicological Junta.

[2] The *"Eroica" Symphony* was originally dedicated to Napoleon, but Beethoven tore up the dedication page in a fit of disgust when he learned that Napoleon had been doing ads for Courvoisier brandy.

modifications that had made this development possible rendered it useless for roping cattle, and within a few decades the American West had replaced Vienna as the cow capital of the world.

Lasso d'amore.

Windbreaker.

(189)

HANSEL AND GRETEL AND TED AND ALICE
an opera in one unnatural act (S. 2^{n-1})
A major; bargain counter tenor/harpsichordist,
beriberitone/calliopist, and piano. (rec. 6)

CAST
QUAINT OLD INNKEEPER
GRETEL RED RIDING HOOD
HANSEL HUNTER
VILLAGE IDIOT
MONK, later revealed to be ALICE ÜBER DEUTSCHLAND
DOCTOR
TEDDY NICE

P. D. Q. rarely received commissions from anyone other than Prince Fred, and he couldn't conceal his surprise when the Vienna Opera Company offered him ten cases of English ale and a fur-lined chamber pot to write something for the 1785-86 season. Nor could he conceal his consternation when he found out, after he had finished writing *Hansel and Gretel and Ted and Alice*, that the Vienna Opera Company consisted of Mr. and Mrs. Fritz Vienna and their little boy, Rudi. There are, as may be ascertained above, seven different roles in the work, and P. D. Q. was afraid at first that he would have to throw it away and write something else if he was ever going to lay his hands on that English

ale, but Herr Vienna, being almost totally deaf, liked the piece and persuaded P. D. Q. to make a few revisions which would make it possible for him and his family to perform the work simply by changing wigs and costumes for each scene, in addition to—and this is one of the most economical innovations in the history of opera—requiring that the singers also play instruments in the Overture and Finale. Several performances were given in the Howdyvolkstheater before the Vienna Opera Company made their final exit late one night, leaving Wein-am-Rhein and many unpaid bills behind them.

Pope Pius VI listed the Monk's infamous aria "Et expecto" as one of the main reasons for his excommunication of P. D. Q. in 1787.

Et expecto resurrecreation;
Et in unum Dominos and checkers;
Qui tollis peccata mundi morning.

Mea culpa kyrie elei-
Sonny Tufts et Allah in Pompeii;
Donna nobis pacem cum what mei;
Agnus and her sister Doris Dei;
Lord, have mercy on my solo.

Et in terra chicken pox romana;
Sic sic transit gloria mañana;
Sanctus estes Kefauviridiana;
In flagrante delicto Svetlana;
Lord, have mercy on my solo.

Credo in, at most, unum deum;
Caveat nabisco mausoleum;
Coitus interruptus bonus meum;
Kimo sabe watchum what you sayum;
Lord, have mercy on my soul so low.

THE ART OF THE GROUND ROUND
(S. 1.19/lb.)
Various keys; three baritones and discontinuo.
(rec. 6 [4th round omitted])

1. Loving is as easy
2. Please, kind sir
3. Jane, my Jane
4. Who, oh who
5. Golly golly oh
6. Nellie is a nice girl

A "ground round" is a round sung over a ground, or repeated bass line. Its use is as old as it is infrequent; one of the earliest notated pieces of English polyphonic music, "Sumer Is Icumen In," is a ground round, although the term itself has not yet found favor with the musicological Establishment, probably simply because of the possibility that P. D. Q. Bach may have coined it.

Most Baroque pieces have a so-called *continuo* part, which consists of a bass line with chord symbols, to be played by one or more bass instruments and a keyboard; the left hand on the keyboard plays the bass line, and the right hand improvises on the basis of the chord symbols. But since, toward the end of his life, P. D. Q. got so fat that he couldn't reach the keyboard with both hands

simultaneously, he simply played the bass line with his left hand and forgot about improvising (which requires a certain amount of thought), or—probably more often—didn't play at all, leaving the bass line to the bass instrument and himself free to drink. He used the term *basso discontinuo* to describe this bastard form of accompaniment.

Generally speaking, the rounds in *The Art of the Ground Round* are of a type fancied by certain seventeenth-century English composers: they reveal, when sung together as rounds, levels of meaning that are not apparent when the parts are sung individually, which is probably just as well, since the polyphonically revealed levels of meaning are sometimes in questionable taste and might have prevented the work's publication had they been immediately obvious on the printed page.

CONCERTO FOR BASSOON VS. ORCHESTRA
(S. 8')
B♭ major.

Break allegro
Not so fast
Rondo alla Turkey Lurkey

The Italians call the bassoon *fagotto*, meaning "bundle of sticks," because people who try to learn to play it often end up using it for firewood instead. The original manuscript of this concerto bears the inscription *Hans Holzmann gewidmet:*[1] when it was unearthed in 1974 the assumption seemed natural that Hans Holzmann was a bassoonist with one of the two orchestras in Wein-am-Rhein, but further research led to the discovery that in fact he was a woodcutter who actually played the first performance of this piece on a bundle of sticks. Although it is not difficult on the bassoon, the concerto makes extraordinary demands on a bundle of sticks, and one can only regret that there are no Hans Holzmänner alive today who would enable us to hear the work as P. D. Q. apparently meant it to be heard.[2]

---

[1] "Dedicated to Hans Holzmann." The French would be *"dédié à Hans Holzmann."*

[2] The often-expressed opinion of Dr. Olaf Johansen of the U. of S.N.D. at H., that "P. D. Q. Bach scores, like children, should be seen and not heard," is not shared by the author.

GRAND SERENADE FOR AN AWFUL LOT
OF WINDS AND PERCUSSION
(S. 1000)
B♭ major; concert band.

Grand entrance
Simply grand minuet
Romance in the grand manner
Rondo mucho grando

P. D. Q. made several sketches for this work, on one of which he used the title *Serenoodle*, but evidently he changed his mind, such as it was, when he wrote out the complete score. The different sketches show that he was also considering various kinds of groups, instrumentationally speaking, but interestingly enough the combination of instruments he ended up using conforms amazingly closely to that of the modern concert band. Some slight adjustments had nevertheless to be made in preparing the recently published performing edition, since certain instruments in the original score, such as the dill piccolo, have become obsolete, and we do not even have any information about their construction. Other instruments, such as the duck call and the police whistle, although now rarely seen on the concert stage, are still readily available and have been retained; as usual, the editor has sacrificed his heroine, Authenticity, only when the gun of Necessity has been held to his head.

The *Grand Serenade for an Awful Lot of Winds and Percussion* was composed on commission for Prince Fred, for some sort of outdoor occasion. P. D. Q. had originally wanted to write a really big work of thirty-five or forty minutes' duration, but he agreed to make it only a third as long when Prince Fred offered to triple the fee. Soon after it was played, a member of the Prince's household used the pages of the score to wrap six large sausages that were sent to Paris to be presented as a gift to Benjamin Franklin, from whom the Prince was anxious to obtain the specifications for building a glass harmonica (see page 11). Eventually the manuscript made its way to an attic in Boston, where the author found it among the belongings of an eighteenth-century Tory, in a box marked "Seditious Material."

3

CONTRITION

WHEN P. D. Q. Bach showed the score of his *Neo-Trio Sonata* to Padre Martini in Wein-am-Rhein, the venerable Italian composer-theoretician-cleric had but one comment: "When does the next coach to Bologna leave?"

Stylistically speaking, the Contrition Period represents an attempt by P. D. Q. to "go home again," to return, as it were, to his musical womb. During his last few days on this earth, he composed as if he were oblivious to all the music he had written since January 1778; such a state of oblivion is certainly more to be envied that censured, and one can hardly blame a dying man for trying to expiate himself, even if his expiations were as bad as his sins.

Cantata: IPHIGENIA IN BROOKLYN
(S. 52, 162)
G major; bargain counter tenor, trumpet mouthpiece, three double reeds, wine bottle, string quartet, and harpsichord. (rec. 1&5 [first movement omitted])

Trumpet involuntary
Aria: "When Hyperion"
Recitative: "And lo!"
Ground: "Dying"
Recitative: "And in a vision"
Aria: "Running"

For more than twenty-five years the two operatic masterpieces by Gluck, *Iphigenia in Aulis* and *Iphigenia in Tauris*, had been regarded as the definitive musical treatments of ancient Greek tragedy in general, and the wanderings of Iphigenia in particular, so it is easy to imagine the controversy that would have been kindled by the first performance of *Iphigenia in Brooklyn* if anyone who had ever heard of Gluck, or for that matter Iphigenia, had been in attendance. Many classical eyebrows *were* raised, however, when in 1963 the author of the present treatise discovered a copy of "Boozey" Hawkes' edition of the cantata in a Liverpool pub, folded up under one of the legs of a table to keep it from wobbling; although Gluck's operas do not loom as high on the cultural horizon as they once did, the fact that among all the Greek scholars of the Western world not *one* seemed to have been aware that Iphigenia had ever gone to Brooklyn struck the ivory towers of countless colleges and universities like a bolt of lightning. The implications of the cantata's libretto, of course, are enormous, and classicologists have been as loath to face them as have Italian-Americans, still reeling from the discovery of Leif Ericsson's Vinland map.

Leaving aside the controversy generated by extramusical considerations, however, *Iphigenia in Brooklyn* is one of P. D. Q. Bach's most popular works among modern concertgoers, due in large part, no doubt, to the spectacular vocal writing. In the eighteenth century most counter tenors (male altos) were one of two kinds: over-the-counter tenors and under-the-counter tenors; P. D. Q., however, preferred the rarer but more versatile bargain counter tenor, whose vocal range, as his name implies, is a real boon to the purse strings, encompassing as it does that of a baritone, tenor, alto, and mezzo-soprano.

P. D. Q. obviously intended the wine bottle part for himself, but since the cantata was premiered posthumously, it was played by Thomas Collins on P. D. Q.'s favorite instrument, a 1783 muscatel.

IPHIGENIA
IN
BROOKLYN

A Cantata for
Bargain Counter Tenor
and Diven Instruments

Composed for Music Lovers,
and also for Connoisseurs,
by

P. D. Q. Bach

Court Organist and Chamber Musician
to His Harness
Prince Fred of Wein-am-Rhein

published at the Sign of the Bottle
by Jonathan Boozey "Hawkes
Liverpool

Oratorio: THE SEASONINGS
(S. 1½ tsp.)
D major; soprano, alto, tenor, bass soloists,
mixed chorus, 2 slide whistles, 2 kazoos, tromboon,
windbreaker & slide windbreaker, shower hose in D,
foghorn, organ, 2 trumpets, timpani, and strings.
(rec. 2; 5 [fugue omitted])

Chorus: "Tarragon of virtue is full"
Recitative: "And there were in the same country"
Duet: "Bide thy thyme"
Fugue: orchestra
Recitative: "Then asked he"
Chorale: "By the leeks of Babylon,
There we sat down, yea, we wept"
Recitative: "Then she gave in"
Aria: "Open sesame seeds"
Recitative: "So saying"
Duet: "Summer is a cumin seed"
Chorus with soloists: "To curry favor, favor curry"

There are speculatory shreds of evidence which suggest that P. D. Q. started composing *The Seasonings* before he left Wein-am-Rhein. For instance, tradition has it that the libretto was written by Prince Fred's cook, Julien Enfant, in French; since we do not possess the original manuscript, and since "Boozey" Hawkes translated everything he published into English, the legend cannot be verified, but we do know that Enfant wrote poetry and took lessons on the dill piccolo from Thomas Pollex, and in a letter to his parents in Rien, dated the 7th of November 1806, he says that he has written the text for a *"cantate culinaire,"* which may indeed have been the genesis of *The Seasonings.*

The presence of a foghorn among the *concertino* instruments (which are otherwise the same as those used in the *Serenude*) may indicate that the oratorio, like Handel's famous *Water Music,* was intended to be performed upon barges on the river; this speculation is supported by the fact that the application form to be filled out by those desiring to sing in the chorus included the question "Are you able to swim?"

DIVERSE AYRES ON SUNDRIE NOTIONS
(S. 99 $\frac{44}{100}$)
Various keys; bargain counter tenor, worm & snake, violin, viola, cello, and harpsichord; also a version for bargain counter tenor and keyboard, with or without cello. (rec. 3 [2nd song omitted])

Sinfonia (in the first version only)
"Do you suffer"
"Hear me through"
"If you have never"

These are the "singing commercials," as we would now call them, that P. D. Q. wrote for use in his traveling medicine show. In a sense they do not belong among the other Contrition Period works, since they were obviously written around the time of the caravan trips (1795–97), but in another sense they do belong here, since they were originally scored only for singer and drum (the latter presumably played by P. D. Q. himself), and it was not until he went to Baden-Baden-Baden that P. D. Q., for some unknown reason probably having something to do with greed, wrote the two arrangements that have survived.

SONATA FOR VIOLA FOUR HANDS
(S. 440)
G major; viola and harpsichord

Andanteeny
Molto fast
Ground round
Allah breve

Although there exists an extensive literature for piano four hands (two people playing at one piano), diligent research has led to the conclusion that this sonata is in all likelihood the only work ever to have been written for two people playing one viola.

The *Sonata for Viola Four Hands* is one of only two or three of the more than a score of P. D. Q. Bach scores that have been discovered which have four movements. If there is any significance to this fact, it has escaped generations of historians, whose

enthusiastic lack of interest in the music of P. D. Q. Bach is openly flaunted in the marketplace, and whose ignorance has been passed down from generation to generation since time immemorial, long before the birth of P. D. Q. Bach gave that ignorance some semblance of justification. Be that as it may, it seems to be true that the forces that go into shaping a typical P. D. Q. Bach composition, of which this is one of the most typical (in its way), are rarely shaped in such a way as to render the final product quadripartite in form, much less in content.

Chorale prelude: "SHOULD"
(S. 365)
G. major; singers, 2 trumpets, timpani, and strings.

Very little is known about this very little work. Judging by its text, it was intended to usher in the New Year; it seems strange, therefore, that it should have been written in May. The fact that he wrote it may indicate that he expected to be around to see the year 1808, but *we* know, even if *he* didn't, that he never made it.

NOTEBOOK FOR BETTY-SUE BACH
(S. 13 going on 14)
Various keys; piano.

Allemande left
Corrate
Oh! Courante!
Two-part contraption
Three-part contraption
Andre Gigue
Traumarei
Capriccio Espagnole for Charles III:
"The Reign in Spain"

Though he completed it during the Contrition Period, P. D. Q. had been working on this collection since the Initial Plunge (see page 167), and his relief upon finishing it is evident in the inscription on the title page (see illustration):

Little Keyboard-Book
for
Betty-Sue Bach
Finished in
Baden-Baden-Baden
in the year 1807
It's about time!

Betty-Sue was extremely moved when P. D. Q. presented her with the work, and she wanted to have it included in the memorial concert of his music that was given in Wein-am-Rhein a month after his death, but since the faster pieces in the collection were beyond her capabilities as a pianist, the *Notebook* was premiered by Porcelina Speck (see page 84), after which the two women got together in a corner and traded stories.

TOOT SUITE
for calliope four hands[1] (S. 212°)
C minor. (rec. 3&5 [3rd mov't.];
6 [2nd mov't.])

Preloud
O.K. chorale
Fuga vulgaris

Steam calliopes, of course, are still seen occasionally in circuses and parades, but in the nineteenth century they were considerably more common, especially at resorts such as Baden-Baden-Baden, and P. D. Q., who was considerably more common himself, could not have been expected to resist writing for such a gross, ear-pummeling instrument.

Until 1972 the original manuscript of the *Toot Suite* eluded discovery, but one of its movements was published anonymously in an 1810 collection entitled *Original Calliope Pieces the Whole World Loves to Play on Their Original Calliopes*, and internal stylistic evidence convinced the author of this tome that the piece, a fugue, was indeed one of the movements of the *Toot Suite*, which P. D. Q. had mentioned in a letter to a friend. After the "Fuga Vulgaris" was recorded (on a small indoor, or chamber, calliope) by the great four-handed organist Emmanuel Pedal, the autograph of the entire work was found underneath a mattress in a circus wagon in Sarasota, Florida; with this discovery, the *Toot Suite* emerged as one of P. D. Q. Bach's most uniquely typical works.

[1] Performing the work on an organ or harmonium seems entirely within the bounds of reasonable authenticity.

THE GROSSEST FUGUE
from The Musical Sacrifice (S. 50% off)
C minor; piccolo, oboe, bassoon, trombone, viola, and contrabass.

It is not known whether or not P. D. Q. completed *The Musical Sacrifice;* this ambitious six-voice fugue is the only part of it that has been found. The idea of the whole work is either an homage to or stolen from *The Musical Offering,* one of Johann Sebastian Bach's last major works, whose thirteen parts are all based on the theme given to Bach by Frederick the Great when Bach visited Potsdam in 1747. The theme, or subject (or theme), of *The Grossest Fugue* was given to P. D. Q. by a burglar who passed through the composer's apartment on his way from robbing the house next door; he had taken more than he could carry, and, as he told

P. D. Q., he didn't think his *Lattenzaun* ("fence") would give him much for the theme anyway, since it was obviously old and had been used a lot.

Fugues have the reputation of being dry and academic, primarily due to the fact (one suspects) that your average layperson has trouble keeping track of where the subject, or theme (or subject) is; P. D. Q. Bach, however, in what can only be described as a didactic *coup,* solves this problem in a novel manner that cannot fail to reach even the densest layperson: he simply instructs each performer to stand up whenever he or she is playing the watchamacallit.

FANFARE FOR THE COMMON COLD
(S. 98.7)
F major; 2 trumpets, 2 horns, and trombone.

Nothing whatsoever is known about this piece, so the author would like to take this opportunity to tell an amusing story he heard the other day: It seems that there was this band of Hungarian vandals roaming around Tibet and molesting the icons in the temples. The government finally decided to declare an all-out war on the vandals, and engaged the services of a retired French general, who happened to be in the area, to direct the conflict. The general had seen the Russian film *Alexander Nevsky*, and he devised a plan to lure the vandals to a frozen-over pond that was used for ice-skating, where he wanted the fighting to take place. The government felt that the general ought to have a title, so on the eve of the battle he was officially named BUDDHA PEST RINK WAR TÊTE. Get it? You may have to say it out loud, sort of quickly.

Canine cantata: WACHET ARF!
("Sleeping Dogs Awake!")
(S. K9)
D major; solo dog, 2 bassoons, 2 horns, 2 trumpets, timpani, and strings.

Entrada
Arietta: "Ach! wo, ach! wo"
Berceuse
Aria: "Bau! Wau!"
Lamento: "Au!"
Finale

Animal vocalists once enjoyed great popularity, but their distinctive singing styles were imitated so extensively by human vocalists (especially opera singers) that they lost their uniqueness and were gradually completely supplanted by their two-legged and more easily toilet-trained rivals. During the heyday of the "animal opera" in the eighteenth century, composers wrote idiomatic but demanding arias not only for dogs (we have already noted the presence of a houndentenor in the cast of *The Stoned Guest*), but for cats, frogs, donkeys, and other animals as well.[1] Now, however, although one may still hear an occasional swan song, the music world seems to have no interest whatsoever in what was once a flourishing *genre*, and finding adequate soloists for revivals of these works is a difficult task indeed. Add to this the fact that engaging an animal to perform in a P. D. Q. Bach piece usually results in extended litigation with the A.S.P.C.A., and the reader may begin to appreciate the problems involved in resurrecting a work such as *Wachet Arf!*

[1] Perhaps the most exotic instance is the title role of Bellini's *La Sonnambula*, which was originally sung by an armadillo.

One of the few contemporary canine singers to gain a large following, Buffy Sainte-Bernard.

4

UNDISCOVERED WORKS

I T will be obvious to even the stupidest reader by now that the massive cover-up conspiracy conducted by the Bach family was only partially successful. For a century and a half P. D. Q. Bach appeared to have been effectively wiped off the slate of history, but since the end of the 1950's, when this author began systematically researching the life and works of the most embarrassing skeleton in the Bach family closet, it has become clear that although much material was destroyed, much managed to escape the effects of "Operation T.O."[1,2]

A careful examination of the surviving data has yielded, in addition to the biographical information presented in this treatise, the names of quite a few works written by P. D. Q. but as yet undiscovered; some of these pieces are undoubtedly permanent victims of the pride-fueled purge perpetrated by an otherwise noble family, but others may yet be brought to light, if not through the humble efforts of the author, perhaps through the even humbler efforts of his students, whose numbers are as constantly increasing by leaps and bounds as they are

---

[1] Total Obliteration.
[2] as "Big" Bertha Bach, a "fodder figure" in Frederick Wilhelm III's army, liked to call it.

regularly decimated by indifference and intimidation.

Most of these works, like the *Neo-Trio Sonata* mentioned on page 166, are known to us by name only. But in certain cases, such as *The Civilian Barber* (see page 180 ff.), some of the music is known, and in one historically important and extremely aggravating case the music was found and then lost again.

In the spring of 1953 the author completed his high school 4H club dissertation on Johann Sebastian Bach's relationship to food, with special emphasis on the *Coffee Cantata*, one of Johann Sebastian's rare ventures into the field of gastronomy. That summer saw the author in Europe searching for the manuscripts of other J. S. Bach cantatas, many of which have never been found, and his poor financial condition forced the author on many occasions to sing for his supper, which, his singing being what it was, usually consisted of stale bread and water. Upon biting into one particularly stiff slice of bread, however, he perceived that what he had at first taken to be spots of black mold were actually musical notes written in a rather tasty ink, and that the bread was not bread at all but was, in reality, a portion of a pile of manuscript pages that had become stuck together and browned with age. Tracing the origin of this serendipitous supper led the author to the ancient Leckendachschloss,[3] in

---

[3] "The Castle of the Leaking Roof." In the eighteenth century its flat roof was covered to a depth of about a foot with finely ground coffee beans; these dried in the sun until the next rainstorm, at which time pots and pans were placed on the floor under the leaks in the roof, and the world's largest coffee-maker was set into operation, providing (after a typical forty-five-minute downpour) enough coffee to keep the entire town of Klatsch awake for a month.

southern Bavaria, where he found the complete manuscript of a *Sanka Cantata*, "by P. D. Q. Bach composed," being employed as a strainer in the caretaker's percolator. A cursory perusal of the music immediately revealed the reason for the atrocious taste of the coffee, but the author's curiosity was piqued by the juxtaposition of such a famous family name and such completely unfamiliar initials, so he purchased the limp and dripping manuscript for a few *Pfennigs* and took it back to the University of Southern North Dakota at Hoople, where he had been engaged to teach in the fall.

Anxious to acquaint himself aurally with, or hear, his recent find, the author carefully dried out the work (which was scored, it turned out, for baritone, violin, and continuo), and arranged for a performance. Unfortunately, however, he made the mistake of inviting the faculty to the final rehearsal, and before the final chord had stopped ringing, Dr. Olaf Johansen, the head of the Voice Department at the University, had run up to the stage, snatched the music, and disappeared out the emergency exit. After a frantic search the author finally found him sitting on the woodpile in back of the science building, calmly enjoying a cigarette and smiling smugly as the fire in the incinerator next to him turned the last page of his loot—the parts the author had copied as well as the original manuscript score—into smoke.

Not since Savonarola burned paintings in the streets of fifteenth-century Florence has such flagrant vandalism been perpetrated in the name of self-righteous artistic morals, and yet the administration of the U. of S.N.D. at H. has steadfastly refused to consider this wanton destruction of an irreplaceable slice of historical life grounds for abrogating Prof. Johansen's tenure and removing him from his position *ex post haste*. Be that as it may, the result of one Philistine professor's irresponsible act of scholarly turpitude is that (barring the remote possibility that other copies were made in P. D. Q. Bach's day) the *Sanka Cantata* now exists only in the memory of those who heard that fateful rehearsal, and in what little smog there is over Hoople, North Dakota. Shortly after the disastrous incident the author wrote down what he could remember of the work, but he does not regard his memory as sufficiently trustworthy to warrant performing or publishing the piece as an authentic P. D. Q. Bach opus.

The martyred manuscript, however, did not die in vain; in spite of its brief, mothlike life, the *Sanka Cantata* did serve the purpose of causing the author to make further inquiries into the darker recesses of the Bach family tree, with the results presented in this modest tome.

Although P. D. Q.'s instrumental music—even that which is known to have been written—has certainly not been completely recovered, there are two other areas of "lost" works which are especially tantalizing; the first of these is opera. *The Stoned Guest, Hansel and Gretel and Ted and Alice,* and the fragments we possess of *The Civilian Barber* represent but a fraction of P. D. Q.'s attacks on musical drama, due to the eclectic, not to say promiscuous, tastes of the manager of the Howdy-volkstheater, Rudolfo Bingo.

In the 1786-87 season Bingo presented no less than two P. D. Q. Bach operas, *The Barren Gypsy* and *Madame Butterbrickle*. Half a decade later the bereaved Norman nobleman Count Pointercount (see page 185) noted in his journal that while he was in Wein-am-Rhein he attended a performance at the Howdyvolkstheater of P. D. Q. Bach's *Rosenkavalier and Guildenstern*, which he found to be an opera "so entrancingly disheveled that I momentarily forgot the sorrow of my dear Thusnelda's passing, God forgive me";[1] in fact, it was after hearing this work that the Count decided to include P. D. Q. among the composers being offered commissions for *The Triumphs of Thusnelda*. He even made a gift to P. D. Q. of the score of Purcell's incidental music to *The Fairy Queen*, no doubt unaware of the fact that giving music to P. D. Q. was a foolproof way of subjecting the composer of said music to plagiarism; if the Count was in Wein-am-Rhein the following year, however, he presumably discovered that fact for himself by attending a performance of *The Dairy Queen*, P. D. Q.'s new "pastoral masque." Finally, P. D. Q.'s favorite bargain counter tenor, Enrico Carouso (see page 100), wrote in a letter to a friend in Vienna that "although I cannot pretend that my enthusiasm is always shared by my audiences, I never tire of singing the 'Queen for a Night' aria from P. D. Q. Bach's *The Magic Fruit*." Thus we have evidence of five operas (and who knows how many more may have been written?) whose obscurity surpasses even that of those that have been discovered.

The other area of "lost" works is even more intriguing: P. D. Q. Bach is known to have written a significant amount of religious music, yet not a single scrap of it seems to have survived. The *Mass in the Allah Mode* has already been mentioned (page 14); the sacrilegiousness of its Near-Eastern influ-

ences, both in terms of religious dogma and musical style, was one of the few things that the Protestant and Roman Catholic clergy agreed upon.[2] The exact role of music in P. D. Q.'s excommunication in 1787 is not clear, but the fact is that he continued to write sacred music after he was severed from the Church (although the *Famous Last Words of Christ* was composed in 1781 or 82, the *Half-Nelson Mass* and the *Missa Hilarious* were apparently written in the 1790's);[3] this fact, which they interpreted as a flaunting of authority, was a source of great consternation to the College of Cardinals, and when, in 1803, P. D. Q. wrote *The Passion According to Hoyle*, all of his religious music was placed on the Index by the Pope, thus categorically precluding its inclusion (unlikely in any case) in any public or institutional library. While it is a well-known fact that many books have gained in popularity as a result of being placed on the Index, in the case of P. D. Q. Bach's religious music the Pope's action appears to have sunk the last nail into the coffin, as it were.[4]

As of this writing P. D. Q. Bach is known to have composed upwards of forty works—hardly an impressive output considering that his creative life

---

[2] In fact Martin Luthifer, the enigmatic pan-universalist who throughout the last decade of the eighteenth century tried to bring about an Ecumenical Council of all Christians, secretly advocated the wide dissemination of P. D. Q. Bach's church music on the theory that it could serve as an "outside enemy" against which all sects would unite. Realizing how gullible P. D. Q. was, he even enlisted the composer's cooperation, promising P. D. Q. the medicine concession if the Council took place.

[3] The notoriously tedious *Boston Mass*, attributed to P. D. Q. by Albrechtsberger, has been shown to be an early but characteristic work of Hummel.

[4] There is always the slight chance that some or all of the

covered a span of thirty years—but during the past
decade and a half very few years have gone by
without the discovery of another peccadillo from
the pen of this "pimple on the face of music," and at
this point a final assessment of his productivity
would, like the infant P. D. Q. himself, have to be
considered ill-conceived or at least premature.

---

manuscripts found their way into the hands of some private
collector of blasphemy, but barring this it seems unrealistic to
entertain high hopes of liberating (to use the current terminol-
ogy) these works from the Black Hole of history, since witches'
covens and other anti-Christ organizations tend to have much
less extensive libraries than do above-ground, Establishment
institutions.

APPENDICES

APPENDIX A

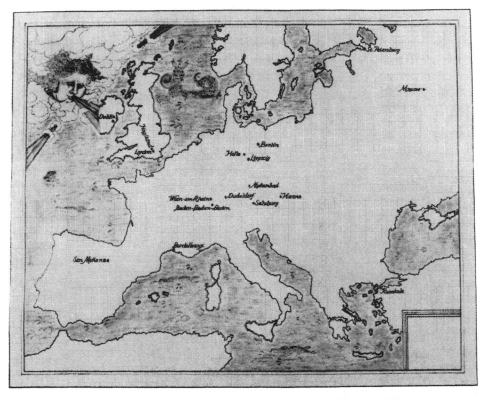

A map showing the places P. D. Q. Bach is known to have visited during his lifetime.

APPENDIX B

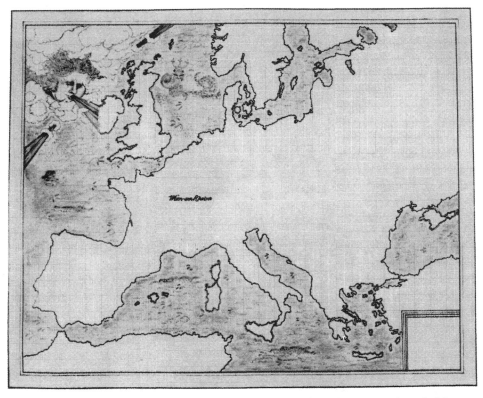

A map showing the places at which public performances of P. D. Q. Bach's music were given during his lifetime.

APPENDIX C

Charles Burney's Account
of His Visit to Wein-am-Rhein in 1788

(This narrative is quoted almost in its entirety since it is one of the few completely reliable references to P. D. Q. Bach that exist.)

I arrived the following day at the town of Wein-am-Rhein, remarkable not only for its intoxicating atmosphere, but also for its extraordinary plumbing system, to my knowledge entirely unique, which by the artful use of subterranean pipes brings hot and cold running wine into every dwelling. I was fortunate in having an introduction to a monk at the local monastery which lay, quite conveniently, very near the entrance to the town, remaining at the same time a respectable distance from it. I soon learned, however, that the intended recipient of my letter was no longer at the monastery, having been exposed as a thief and sent away with a brand on his forehead signifying to all the world that he was a felonious monk. He with whom I spoke—a certain Brother Bruder—seemed to be a helpful sort of fellow, so at length I inquired whether he could inform me as to the whereabouts of the composer P. D. Q. Bach, who I had heard was residing in the nearby town.

Upon mention of that name, the monk's face darkened and his eyes rolled toward heaven as he crossed himself thrice. He confided to me that in the long history of the Church, P. D. Q. Bach is the only *person* ever to have been declared a cardinal

sin. He said that if all churchmen worshipped the Lord as zealously as P. D. Q. Bach worshipped the bottle, there never would have been a Reformation. Naturally I had the greatest respect for the piety of this man of the cloth, a respect which was, however, somewhat diminished when I learned that he himself performed the communion service ten times a day, every day, even when he ran out of bread.

(Burney then discovered that Padre Martini was at the monastery (see page 90), and the two men chatted about various matters that do not concern us here. Eventually Burney proceeded to town and located an address for P. D. Q. that had been given to him by the Padre.)

Upon entering, I discovered that it was a tavern, which was of considerable surprise to me, since it was one of the largest and most awe-inspiring buildings in town. I told the keeper whom I sought, and he told me that I would find his "best customer," as he put it, sitting at the head of the table in the back room.

It was with the keenest sense of anticipation and not a little difficulty that I made my way through the front room—walking on the tabletops seemed to be the quickest way—and into the room at the rear. There at the head of the table, surrounded by friends and steins (there were, I think, about five friends and about fifty steins) sat the object of my search, dipping a quill pen in a glass of wine and applying it to a sheet of music paper. He seemed to be an extremely short man, with indelicate features and a complexion which, were he to bathe in the Red Sea, would surely render him invisible. The impression of shortness, it turned out, was due to the fact that he had fallen off his chair and was hanging on the table by his chin; his colleagues, if

that is the correct word for the large noses that surrounded him, assured me that he was rarely above the table at all, and that most of his composing was done on the floor.

(Unfortunately P. D. Q. passed out shortly after Dr. Burney entered the room; the latter decided to wait for him to come to, but after two days gave up and continued his journey; his description of the visit ends with an interesting observation):

Wein-am-Rhein is a paradoxical town, for its population is peaceful, yet in a constant state of ferment.

APPENDIX D
Bibliography

Carouso, Enrico, *Music Minus Two: My Life As a Castrato,* translated from the Italian by Lorenzo da Ponte (New York, 1835).

Classic Comics, *Born To Make Music! The Story of Big John Bach and His Outasite Organ!* (Story: Stan Lee; Art: Jack Pollack; Lettering: Learned Hand) (New York, 1961).

Collins, Thomas, *Pipes and Ale: The Memoirs of Thomas Collins* (Edinburgh, 1809).

Grey, Zane, *Riders of the Purple Sage* (New York, 1912).

Hans, David, "Bach! Humbug!", in the *Musical Hindquarterly,* xvii.

Pointercount, Count, *My Very Own Diary* (London, 1811).

Scheibe, Johann Adolph, *Big Deal: J. S. Bach As I Knew Him,* translated from the German by Cordell Hull (Washington, D.C., 1943).

Youngman, Henny, *Music in the Eighteenth Century,* Hutchins' College Outline Series (Chicago, 1973).

APPENDIX E

IV. Two-Part Contraption

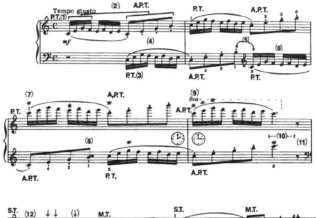

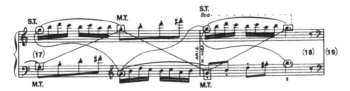

NOTEBOOK FOR BETTY-SUE BACH, © 1967, 1973, WHITE BEAR PRODUCTIONS. USED BY PERMISSION.

(222)

Analysis of the Two-Part Contraption

(From the *Notebook for Betty-Sue Bach*)

P.T. = Principal Theme   A.P.T. = Assistant Principal Theme
S.T. = Second Theme   M.T. = Minute Theme

COMMENTS

(1) The Principal Theme consists of eight notes; the second group of four is a figuration called a *cambiata* (literally, "moneychanger," whose street-cry in sixteenth-century Rome began with this configuration of notes), using the same pitches as those used in the first group, except that a D is used instead of a C, and there is no G.

(2) The Assistant Principal Theme has four notes, the first three of which are a rhythmic augmentation of the first three notes of the Principal Theme; the fourth note is the same as the fourth note of the Principal Theme, transposed up an augmented fourth.

(3) The second voice (left hand) enters in canon (corruption of Spanish word for "canyon," i.e., the second voice is lower, or deeper, than the first). It repeats the melodic material of the first voice, but not at the same time.

(4) The juxtaposition of staccato notes in the right hand and legato notes in the left hand is an amusing touch.

(5) This stunning leap from the space above the staff to the ledger line below it is softened somewhat by the presence of the treble clef, but it is still a daring device, used no doubt to break the strictness of the imitation.

(6) Another way of introducing variety: in the second appearance in the left hand of the Principal Theme the note stems go up instead of down.

(7) That the piece should be played heroically is proved by an examination of the notes in measures 3 and 4 marked with an asterisk, which, allowing for the transposition from E♭ major to C major, are identical with the first eight notes of the opening theme of Beethoven's "*Eroica*" Symphony.

(8) The "leading tone" is the most important note in the scale, just as the "leading lady" or the "male lead" is the most important performer in a dramatic production, and, like its thespian counterparts it always goes up (to avoid being "upstaged" by other notes), never down. Adding an arrow to the note head to indicate this proclivity coincidentally produces the symbol for masculinity, and indeed the "leading tone" exhibits its many aggressive traits commonly associated with the male of the species (Counterpoint).

(9) 8va: from the French; literally, "eight goes," indicating that the eighth notes in the previous half measure of the right hand part are gone.

(10) In this brief section the canon is at the unison, both intervalically and rhythmically.

(11) During this rest, common to both parts, the music modulates from the key of the tonic, which is the dominant key of a piece, to that of the dominant, a key introduced to provide a tonic effect, a refreshing change.

(12) The Second Theme is introduced, as is customary, in the dominant key; typically, too, it is of a contrasting nature with respect to the Principal Theme: note that only two of its pitches (indicated by arrows) appear in the Principal Theme (measure 1), and that it makes much more extensive use of ledger lines as an expressive device.

(13) The vertical, or "lazy," unlaut surrounding the fourth line is an anachronism; it is a holdover from the days of the *Meistersinger* (and even earlier—the era of the musical elf, or Minisinger), when it indicated that all vowels on the fourth line were to be palatalized.

(14) The rest in the left hand is to be performed on the beat, not before, as in later practice.

(15) P. D. Q. Bach obviously did not realize the potential of this three-note motif, used so effectively by Brahms in the first movement of his *Second Symphony*.

(16) Fortunately, at this point the right hand is in the treble clef and the left hand is in the bass clef; if both hands were in the same clef, there would be an excruciating dissonance here.

(17) Connecting the G's (circled) of the Second Theme, and doing the same with those (boxed) of the Minute Theme, we see the symmetry of the melodic structure revealed, as well as the essential unity of the two seemingly disparate themes. Also, concentrating on these Foreground Notes we see that both themes are basically elaborations of the famous "V for Victory" motif (··· —) thought by many to be the exclusive province of Beethoven and Morse.

(18) Note that these rests have not been transposed; they are exactly the same as those at the end of measure 4. Here too they are used for modulation, this time from the dominant back to the tonic.

(19) There follows (not shown here) an extended recapitulation of the Principal Theme Group, during which the manuscript breaks off. Why P. D. Q. left the piece unfinished we do not know, but we may surmise that it was because either the manuscript paper or he himself fell to the floor while the fourteenth measure was being written out, and there the matter lay.

APPENDIX F

Discography

All the recordings are on the Vanguard label, and are available at indiscriminate record stores throughout the United States and Canada and even in certain foreign countries whose balance-of-payments deficits are especially large.

(1) The Music of P. D. Q. Bach (Peter Schickele Town Hall Concert) VSD-79195. Chamber orchestra conducted by Jorge Mester.

Concerto for Horn and Hardart (Froelich, Schickele)
Cantata: *Iphigenia in Brooklyn* (Ferrante)
Quodlibet (by Prof. Schickele)
Sinfonia Concertante (Eisenstadt, Lewis, Buetens, Lickman, Zolotareff, Schickele)

(2) An Hysteric Return: P. D. Q. Bach at Carnegie Hall VSD-79223. Jorge Mester conducting the Royal P. D. Q. Bach Festival Orchestra.

Oratorio: *The Seasonings* (Haywood, Kleinman, Ferrante, Woolf, the Okay Chorale)
"Unbegun" Symphony (by Prof. Schickele)
Pervertimento for Bagpipes, Bicycle, and Balloons (Eisenstadt, Schickele, Lewis)

(3) P. D. Q. Bach on the Air (Report from Hoople) VSD-79268. Prof. Schickele conducting I Virtuosi di Hoople, with John Ferrante, bargain counter tenor.

Echo Sonata for Two Unfriendly Groups of Instruments
"Do you suffer" (from *Diverse Ayres on Sundrie Notions*)
New Horizons in Music Appreciation (Beethoven Fifth Symphony Sportscast) (Schickele, Dennis)
Traumarei for Unaccompanied Piano (Seifenblase)
Schleptet in E♭ Major
What's My Melodic Line? (Quiz)
"Fuga Vulgaris" (from the *Toot Suite*) (Pedal)
"If you have never" (from *Diverse Ayres on Sundrie Notions*)

(4) The Stoned Guest VSD-6538. John Nelson conducting the Orchestra of the University of Southern North Dakota at Hoople Heavy Opera Company

The Stoned Guest: half-act opera (complete) (Haywood, Kleinman, Ferrante, Bernice, Schickele)
Two Madrigals from *The Triumphs of Thusnelda* "The Queen to Me a Royal Pain Doth Give" "My Bonnie Lass She Smelleth" (Haywood, Kleinman, Ferrante, Nelson, Schickele)

(5) The Wurst of P. D. Q. Bach (selections
from the first four albums)
VSD-719/20, VSQ-40007/8 (quad). Artists as
above.

Concerto for Horn and Hardart
Cantata: Iphigenia in Brooklyn
New Horizons in Music Appreciation (Beethoven
Sportscast)
Schleptet in Eb Major
What's My Melodic Line?
"My Bonnie Lass She Smelleth" (from The
Triumphs of Thusnelda)
"Unbegun" Symphony (last movement only)
Half-act opera: The Stoned Guest (highlights)

"Fuga Vulgaris" (from the Toot Suite)
Oratorio: The Seasonings (fugue omitted)

(6) The Intimate P. D. Q. Bach
VSD-79335, VSQ-40016 (quad). The
Semi-Pro Musica Antiqua (Ferrante, Oei,
Nelson, Schickele).

Hansel and Gretel and Ted and Alice: opera in
one unnatural act
"The O.K. Chorale" (from the Toot Suite)
"Erotica" Variations
The Art of the Ground Round

APPENDIX G

Glossary of Unusual Instruments
Used by P. D. Q. Bach

Balloons. See *Pervertimento,* page 177.

Bicycle. See *Pervertimento,* page 177.

Calliope. A loud, mobile organ whose tones are produced by steam-blown whistles. Most authorities state that the instrument was invented in America in the 1880's, but they are dead wrong; almost a century earlier a professional water boiler in Badenweiler on the edge of the Black Forest built a *Dampforgel* (steam organ), the first of several models, all of which became quite popular throughout Europe. *(Toot Suite, Hansel and Gretel and Ted and Alice)*

Double Reed Hookah in F. One of the few three-player instruments ever invented. Like that of the piccolo, its range does not go very low, but you can get very high on it. *(Perückenstück)*

Double reed slide music stand. A wire music stand, minus the actual rack, is held upside down; the reed and bocal (tube) are inserted into the hole on the bottom, and the adjustable part of the stem is used like a trombone slide. Its pitch range is about a minor third; its expressive range, however, is more limited. *(Sinfonia Concertante)*

Foghorn. Little is known about eighteenth-century foghorns. P. D. Q. may have had in mind a large conch shell, blown like a trumpet. Lacking more definitive information, however, using a hand-held compressed gas foghorn for modern performances seems quite justified. *("Erotica" Variations, The Seasonings)*

Hardart. See Concerto for Horn and Hardart, page 173.

Kazoo. The kazoo is the modern form of an old instrument called the *mirliton,* which consisted of a pipe with a membrane over one end into which one sang; in the seventeenth century it was known as the *flûte-eunuque* and was much admired for its uniquely eunuchal tone quality. If you don't believe me, look it up in the Harvard Dictionary of Music. *(Serenude, "Erotica" Variations, The Seasonings)*

Lasso d'amore. See *"Erotica" Variations,* page 188.

Left-handed sewer flute. A leaden flute which is played left-handed, giving it its characteristic "left-handed" tone quality. *(Gross Concerto, Sinfonia Concertante)*

Nose flute. Like the handkerchief, the nose flute is held up to the nose and blown into; unlike the handkerchief, it produces a clear, whistle-like tone that is quite pleasing and not at all nasal. A professional engagement playing this instrument is referred to as a "nose job."

Ocarina. A globular flute, often colloquially

called a "sweet potato." Its most usual shape is that of a horizontal tear from an extraordinarily large eye. **Grosse ocarina.** A grosser form of the same instrument. *(Gross Concerto, Sinfonia Concertante)*

Oscar Mayer wiener whistle. Measuring about two inches raw, this member of the fipple flute family is surely the smallest instrument (as well as the tastiest) ever to be accompanied by an orchestra. *(Gross Concerto)*

Police trombone. The *Polizeiposaune* produces the attention-getting sound of a siren simultaneously with the attention-getting sound of a trombone. It was often placed at the head of parade bands in order to help clear the way. *(Perückenstück,* Suite from *The Civilian Barber)*

Pumpflute. Two people are necessary to play the *Pumpenflöte:* one to finger the notes and another to man or woman the pump. *(Perückenstück)*

Shower hose in D. P. D. Q. Bach rarely bathed, at least in water, and he undoubtedly reasoned that since he didn't use his shower hose for showering, he might as well use it for something else. Its tone is cleaner than that of the French horn, which in other respects it resembles to an upsetting degree. *(Serenude, The Seasonings)*

Slide whistle. The slide whistle has been called a poor man's trombone. Like the kazoo, it is nowadays mostly thought of, when it is thought of at all, as little more than a toy. In spite of its large range it is little more than a toy. *(Gross Concerto, Serenude, "Erotica" Variations, The Seasonings)*

Snake. The snake, so called because it is capable of playing all the scales, produces two distinct kinds

of tone at the same time, in addition to a menacing rattle. Closely related to the worm, it is rarely seen today except in museums and woodpiles. *(Diverse Ayres on Sundrie Notions)*

Tonette. A cheap, synthetic recorder with amusing pretensions. *(Gross Concerto)*

Tromboon. A cross between a trombone and a bassoon, combining all the disadvantages of both into one convenient instrument. *(Serenude, The Seasonings)*

Windbreaker. The windbreaker consists of a series of tuned mailing tubes, which accounts for the rather puzzling name by which it is known in some of the eighteenth-century orchestration treatises: the mailing tuba. It does not, however, account for the instrument's extremely unusual tone quality, about which the less said the better. The **slide windbreaker,** on the other hand, has two nesting tubes which enable the player to *glissando* (slide) from one note to another, but it doesn't help. *(Serenude, "Erotica" Variations, The Seasonings)*

Wine bottle. Each successive movement of the cantata *Iphigenia in Brooklyn* requires a lower pitch from the wine bottle than the preceding movement. Obviously the main difficulty in performing the wine bottle part is not the actual production of the sound, which is accomplished by blowing across the open end of the bottle; what separates the experienced wine bottlist from the mere "social player" is the ability to finish the piece in anything resembling an upright position. Since a complete performance of the work entails imbibing an entire bottle of what is likely, given the economics of the classical concert scene, to be an unmistakably inexpensive red wine in the space of ten minutes or less, it is to be expected that even virtuosi are often unable to leave the stage without assistance.

Worm. The worm is an unusually unusual instrument in that its pitch is determined by where it is pinched. The utilization of this pitch-pinch relationship in a wind instrument is, to the author's knowledge, entirely unique, and not to be encouraged.

APPENDIX H

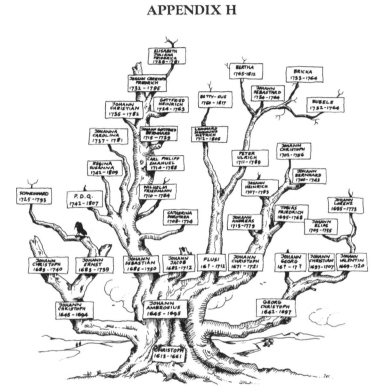

The Bach Family Tree

Female members of the family are included where information is available, but children who did not survive infancy have been omitted. The line descending from Johann Ambrosius' daughter Flusi has been extended an extra generation to include several persons who figure in the text, and also because the additional data thereby provided is difficult if not virtually impossible to find in traditional, male-oriented genealogies.

INDEX

Important references are given in boldface. Italicized numbers indicate fleeting references, whereas numbers in parentheses refer to mere implications or unwarranted extrapolations. Asterisks are used to identify particularly distasteful passages.

a, 53
acute, 16
Adler, Molly, 93
ago, two hundred years, 26, 62
Albrechtsberger, Johann Georg, 210
Armand, Marie, 36
avoid, 54

b, 53
Bach, A. M., *3*, 4-5, 36, (38)
Bach, B., 138
Bach, "B." B., 208
Bach, B. "B.," 144
Bach, B., 40
Bach, B.-S., *12*, 66, (108), 110, 112, 116, 121, 202
Bach, C. G., 4, (38)
Bach, C. P. E., 5, 11, *12*, (38)
Bach, D., 138
Bach, E., 136
Bach, E. J. F., 40
Bach, G. B., 4, (38)
Bach, G. H., 4, (38), 40
Bach, J. A. A., 40
Bach, J. C., 4, 40, 44

Bach, J. C., 5, *10*, 11, 14, 15, (38), 40, 56, 58-62, 146
Bach, J. C. F., 11, (38), 40
Bach, J. S., vii, (ix), (xiii), 3*, 4-5, *6*, 11, 15-18, 30*, 32, 34, 36, *38*, 40, 44, 48, *90*, *112*, 166, 204, 208, 221
Bach, L., 42
Bach, L. S. D., 11-12, 66
Bach, M. B., (3)
Bach, P. D. Q., **iii,** vii et al.
Bach, P. U., *12*, (38)
Bach, R. S., 11, (38), 40
Bach, S., 10-11, 14, (38)
Bach, "S." B., 58
Bach, T. F., *10*, (38)
Bach, T. T. F., 40
Bach, W. F., 3, 4, *8*, 38
Bach, W. F. E., 112*
Bach, Z., 127
Bartók, Béla, *159*
beard, 44, 123
Beethoven, Ludwig, 12, 96, *182*, 188
Beethoven, Moe, 96
Behrer, Paul, 188
Bellini, Vincenzo, 206

Speck, Porcelina, 84, 202
Spitoony, Phil, 82
straw
    drinking, 74
    final, 12
strings, apron, 13

Telemann, Georg Philipp, 166
Tell, William, 121
ten, 15, 19
tenure, *viii*, 121
the Great, Catherine, 14
the Great, Frederick, 16, 17-18
the Insignificant, Ferdinand, 7-9, 106
thought, food for, xi, (11)
Tufts, Sonny, 191

unbelievable, 92
under, had lain submerged, 24
underbelly, soft, vii

van Swieten, Gottfried, 15-18, 70
VI, Pope Pius, 190
view, another, 127
Vivaldi, Antonio, 166
von Brandigburg, Bernhard Erich, 3
von Kayserling, Count, 7
von Schrumpfennase, Countess, 17-18
von Trio, Archduke, 8
von Tutti, "Cozy," 70, 72, 76

Walburga, Bishop, 100, 102, 104
Waller, Fats, *165*

XIV, Pope Clement, 11

Youngman, Henny, 221

Zahnstocher, Kleiner, 6, 8, 9*
Zahnstocher, Ludwig, 6-9, *12*, 13, 50, 52, 88, 106
Zall, Anton, 93

About the Author

Prof. Peter Schickele is extremely closely related to the serious composer Peter Schickele, who was born in Ames, Iowa, in 1935 and raised in Iowa, Washington, D.C., and Fargo, North Dakota. His principal composition studies were with Sigvald Thompson, Roy Harris and Vincent Persichetti. After earning degrees at Swarthmore College and the Juilliard School of Music he spent a year in Los Angeles as Composer-in-Residence on a Ford Foundation grant, following this with four years of teaching, mostly at Juilliard. Since 1965 he has been a free-lancer, involved in many different areas of composition: symphonic (including commissioned works for the St. Louis Symphony and the Louisville Orchestra); film (documentaries and four feature films, including *Crazy Quilt* and *Silent Running*); TV (including several Sesame Street segments); theater (as a member of the chamber rock group The Open Window he was one of the composer-lyricists for the Broadway hit *Oh! Calcutta!*); in addition to choral and chamber music. He has worked as arranger-conductor for several recording artists, among them Joan Baez; for one of her albums, *Baptism*, he also composed all the music. In spite of the heavy concert schedule of his relative Prof. Schickele (with whom he is on very good terms), Mr. Schickele finds time to write and perform his own music all over the country as well as in New York City, where he lives with his wife Susan (a children's dance teacher) and their children, Karla and Matthew.

Made in the USA
San Bernardino, CA
05 August 2019